How to Grow and Use Herbs

OTHER CONCORDE GARDENING BOOKS

How to Grow and Use Herbs

Ann Bonar
and
Daphne MacCarthy

Ward Lock Limited · London

© Ward Lock Limited 1974

Paperback ISBN 07063 1669 X

First published in Great Britain 1974
by Ward Lock Limited, 116 Baker Street,
London, W1M 2BB, a Pentos Company

Reprinted 1976
Reprinted 1977
Reprinted 1979

Designed by John Munday

Text set in IBM Press Roman
by Preface Ltd,
Salisbury, Wiltshire
Printed and bound in Great Britain by
Cox & Wyman Ltd, London, Fakenham and Reading

Contents

1
Herbs in the Garden

What is a herb? Most people regard a herb as a special type of plant, part of which is used in cooking to add another flavour or help emphasise one already there. However, when you begin to think about it, the word can cover a very wide range of plants – one could say that all herbaceous plants are herbs. The dictionary or botanical definition of a herb is: 'any plant with a soft or succulent stem or stems that dies to the roots every year', but in general any herbaceous or woody plant which is aromatic in one or more of its parts and which is considered to have culinary, medicinal or cosmetic value, can be regarded as a herb.

Herbs can be classified in a variety of different ways and any one or more of these can be pursued if the herb virus gets a hold of you. You can devote yourself to making as complete a collection as possible of the herbs used in cooking. Suggested kinds to start with are the big five: parsley, mint, thyme, chives and sage; from these you can expand to include marjoram, garlic, fennel, rosemary, sorrel, tarragon, angelica and the savories. From there you can go on to the herbs used in making teas, wines and drinks in general – there is no end to the ways in which the cook can make use of herbs.

You could concentrate on the medicinal kinds, though if you want to use them for curing ailments of various kinds, be extremely careful in consulting reliable literature, and make sure that you are using the right plants. The plant family *Umbelliferae* contains several herbs, which are rather alike in general appearance, including hemlock which of course provides a deadly poison! It is interesting, though, to discover the old plants that were once much used by doctors; many were useless but a few were effective, and the foxglove for instance is still grown to provide digitalin for use in heart complaints. The autumn crocus (*Colchicum*), comfrey, betony, aconitum, poppy, and belladonna are also all considered to be medicinal herbs.

Some people prefer to collect plants in botanical groups, and herbs lend themselves rather well to this; for instance to take the family *Umbelliferae* again, it contains a good many useful herbs such as lovage, fennel, coriander, and dill, and the *Labiatae* is another, with basil, balm, hyssop and marjoram counted among its members. Each family can have a bed devoted to it, and it is easy then, and rather surprising, to see how widely plants can differ within a family in habit, shape of leaf and even apparently in flower, though a trained botanist will be able to pinpoint the similarities on which the classification is based. Collections of this kind can be seen at Kew, Cambridge and the Chelsea Physic Garden – the last mentioned is, however, only open for students and professional use.

Another way of collecting herbs is to grow only those which are pleasantly aromatic or perfumed; this would of course mean no parsley, no garlic, no savory and so on, but it does leave room for quite a lot more plants, such as lavender, thyme, lemon balm, basil and mint. Some need bruising before releasing their fragance, and growing them on paths or at the edges of beds close to paths, will ensure the necessary pressure.

One of the nicest and most satisfying ways to grow herbs is to collect them together into a small garden within a garden. It is much easier, then, to give them the special attention and conditions that they like. Most of them prefer sun and shelter from from wind, and the kind of soil vegetables do best in. Paving seems to lend itself to herbs, as it gives definition to their sometimes rather untidy growth, and it can be used in a kind of chess board pattern or laid out like the spokes of a wheel. The carpeting herbs can take the place of paving, such as creeping thyme or chamomile, if paving is unobtainable.

Hedges round the herb garden will help to shelter it, or climbers trained up trellis work or similar supports; the hedges can be of herbs themselves such as lavender, rosemary, sage, sweet bay (slow to grow) or *Rosa gallica officinalis,* the Apothecaries' rose, If the garden is to be laid out in a square it could have a bed in each corner, with a centre such as a pool, sundial, or bird bath. A seat in the centre or to one side will always be popular, so that the fragrance and aroma of the herbs can be enjoyed; there is a certain old world peacefulness about a herb garden, too, which is best absorbed by lingering. If you have cats, they will nearly always be found in it somewhere peacefully asleep, knowing that they are least likely to be disturbed there. Beware, however, if

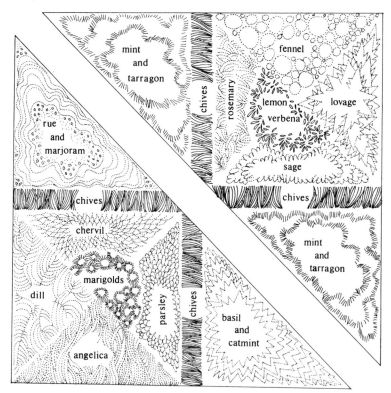

8

you plant nepeta (catmint) — the peace will not be quite so absolute, as the cats tear it to pieces in their attempts to become one with it.

However you decide to lay out your herb garden, try to design it on paper beforehand. Then you can be sure of blending the colours of foliage and flowers, and avoid the mistake of planting tall herbs in front of the mound-forming kinds. Some herbs have beautifully coloured leaves; others have an architectural habit of growth with handsomely shaped leaves; some die down completely in winter, others have attractive flowers and all this should be taken into account when designing a herb garden. One needs to know, too, the amount of space a plant will take up in girth as well as height. Make sure that herbs which like the same conditions of growth all grow together.

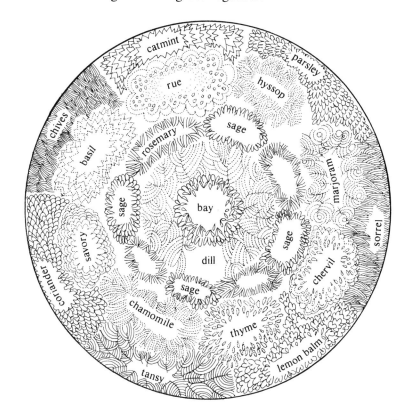

An even more elaborate form of herb garden is one laid out as the Elizabethan knot gardens used to be. These consisted of intricate arrangements of small beds separated by low growing hedges, or paths of coloured stones or sand. Box (*Buxus suffruticosa sempervirens*) makes a good low dividing hedge, though not considered a true herb; others are santolina (lavender cotton), sage or artemisia. There is a typical Elizabethan knot garden laid out at Hampton Court, and another at New Place, Stratford-upon-Avon.

For those who would like the effect of a lawn in a herb garden, a good substitute for grass is chamomile, which will stand a certain amount of walking on, and will not need much cutting, perhaps three or four times during spring and summer. It makes a good green carpet, as do also creeping thyme, penny-royal and the creeping mint *Mentha requienii.* Paths within the herb garden can be covered with these plants as an alternative to paving or bricks; walking on them will help to release their aromatic perfumes, as the leaves and stems are bruised by the pressure.

Three famous herb gardens which will give you an idea of what can be achieved are those at Sissinghurst Castle, Knole near Sevenoaks, and Lullingstone Castle, near Eynsford, all in Kent; they are open to the public and the first two are National Trust gardens.

Besides growing herbs in their own garden, they can be given a separate border, like a herbaceous border. The same principles of design will apply to this as to the herbaceous kind, in that tall plants are better at the back, and plants should be grown closely enough to prevent weeds establishing themselves. Good front-of-border plants are things like the golden-leaved marjoram, chives, parsley and thyme. The rounded, bushy, middle-of-the-border plants are hyssop, sorrel, lemon balm, pot marjoram, tarragon and verbena, and for giving height and architectural quality, angelica, fennel, and lovage can be used. Facing the sun, and with a tall hedge as backing, a herb border can look very ornamental as well as being useful, particularly if some of the medicinal herbs are included, such as foxglove, lily of the valley and poppies whose flowers are more showy than those of the purely culinary herbs.

10

Since the majority of herbs are grown for cooking, another good site would seem to be the vegetable garden, giving them a permanent small border to themselves, alongside the vegetables. The perennial herbs will obviously stay in the same place for some years, but those which are annual and are grown afresh from seed every year, will need freshly prepared soil each year, and so take a little more time and attention.

Still, this can be done at the same time as the ground is prepared for vegetable sowing. Herb seeds are sown in drills, and thinned, as vegetables are, and will need hoeing to remove weeds, and watering in dry weather, with occasional applications of liquid fertilisers. Try to make sure that a part of the vegetable garden is chosen which supplies the conditions of sun, shelter, and well-drained soil mentioned previously.

Obviously, one of the best places to grow cooking herbs is as near the kitchen as possible. There is nothing more irritating than getting halfway through a recipe and discovering that you have forgotten to pick the particular herbs needed for it, and then having to go to the end of the garden for them. It is always a dark night, pouring with rain, when this happens, and it is terribly tempting, then, to do without. At least if they are just outside the backdoor, they are quick to get if you have forgotten to pick in advance.

An even more convenient way to grow just a few different kinds of herbs is in the form of 'mobile' herbs, that is in window boxes, pots, hanging baskets and miniature gardens. They can then be moved about and given the best possible position for light and sun. Soil mixtures, feeding and watering can be tailored to fit their requirements exactly, and it ensures that garden-less cooks can not only have their own home grown herbs, but can also have them at any time. Quite a few herbs which will not survive our winters out of doors can be retained all the year round in this way. Balconies, outer window sills and roof gardens can be pressed into use; inside window ledges which get plenty of light are excellent.

2
Herbs and their Cultivation

The joy about herb gardening is that it is easy. Herbs are not faddy plants which demand, for instance, such niceties as acid soil, regular feeding, a lot of manure, shade at midday, mulching with oak leaves, and so on. They do like shelter from wind but what plant, or person for that matter, does not like protection from all the gales that blow? Given a reasonably average soil, they should all grow perfectly well, and indeed often the trouble is, as with vegetables, they produce far more vegetation than one can comfortably use. Still, if they are being grown mainly for ornament, even this will not matter.

Probably most important of all is to choose the right position in the garden. Somewhere facing south and/or west, with a barrier against the north east winds, and some kind of screen to break the force of the south west gales of summer, will make a very good site for herbs. If the ground slopes a little towards the sun, it is even better, but this is not so important. Try to avoid a part of the garden which tends to remain frozen long after other parts have thawed; many herbs are natives of the hills and coasts of the Mediterranean and are used to baking heat in summer and dry winters with little if any frost. Actually, it is not so much low temperatures, as the alternation of cold and warmth in winter combined with constant damp which we get in Britain, that is responsible for killing plants.

If there is a suitably sunny position, but no barriers to wind, a temporary screen of hessian or wattle fencing will provide this, while a hedge grows up. Even trellis work or strands of wire will be effective, if climbing plants such as sweetpeas, nasturtiums, runner beans or ornamental hops are grown over them.

The hedge can be formal or informal, tall to give a completely enclosed garden, or low growing, in the pattern of the Elizabethan knot garden. The plants forming the hedge need not be herbs, though there are some very good ones for this, for instance, rosemary, *Rosa gallica*, and sage.

Soil which becomes sodden in winter or after prolonged rain must have its ability to drain water away improved. This can be done by forking in coarse sand while preparing the soil, 3-4 lb per sq yd. Peat will help the soil particles to form into crumbs, and so help to make room for air and water to circulate. It can be mixed in at the rates the suppliers suggest; leafmould at 7 lb per sq yd, or rotted garden compost at a lower rate because it contains more plant food. For heavy soils these preparations can be made during the late autumn or early winter. Soil which is already quick to dry out will only need the addition of organic matter, a month or so before sowing or planting. If mixed into a soil earlier, it is in fact liable to be washed out by the winter rains.

If the soil is really short of plant food, as town garden or old garden soils often are, you must give some kind of artificial fertiliser before sowing or planting. Herbs are said not to require a particularly fertile soil, but it is no good expecting them to do well if the growing medium is dead, that is, if there is neither mineral nutrient or humus in it.

Some people will say that artificial fertilisers should never be used, but in some soils plants will never get going without them no matter how much humus is put in. Once the soil fertility has been built up and the soil brought to life again, by feeding and manuring and regular cultivation, then it may be possible to do without powder and granulated fertilisers, and rely completely on a little mulching (spreading a surface layer) with compost, leafmould, or peat.

In short, preparation of the soil before planting herbs

should consist either of adding coarse sand and peat/ leafmould/compost or similar material if drainage is bad, in late autumn, or it should consist of mixing in organic matter about a month before planting or sowing. In both cases fertiliser can be given ten days or so before sowing or planting at 2-3 oz per sq yd., raking it into the top 2 or 3 in. or so.

A word about compost making here. Compost heaps first came on the scene when a shortage of farm manure began to be apparent, as horse-drawn ploughs were replaced by tractors and as towns became bigger and more distant from sources of supply. Whereas farm manure is mainly animal organic matter, compost is mainly vegetable in origin, containing rotted down leaves, soft stems, flowers, grass cuttings, in fact all kinds of soft vegetation; household refuse can also be included such as tea leaves, orange skins, potato peelings and so on. The ideal size of the heap is about 5 x 4 x 5 ft.

Such a heap heats up rapidly and to a considerable temperature if built quickly, using the above materials, with the addition of a sprinkling of lime alternating with a sprinkling of nitrogenous fertiliser on every 6-in layer of vegetation. A very wet or dry heap will not rot, and adjustments must be made to either condition.

A heap started in spring should be ready for use about six to eight weeks after completion; one started in mid-summer probably will take all the winter to rot down completely to a dark brown crumbly substance. Complete rotting of the heap will be assisted if it can be raised off the ground slightly so that there is air beneath it, which will be drawn up through the centre. If the heap is built up round posts, their removal when the heap is finished will improve ventilation even more. Wooden slats or wire netting will help to keep the heap tidy; for small gardens wire bins can be obtained which are easily dismantled and packed flat when not wanted.

The benefit to the ground which results from using compost material made in this way is out of all proportion to the quantities added. The bacteria and worms contained in it continue to live, feed and work not only in the compost but in the soil also, water and air become much more mobile, particles of plant food dissolve in the soil moisture much more readily, so there is more nutrient for roots to absorb, and so on and so on. The end product of compost-treated soils cannot help but be better herbs in all respects, whether healthier, stronger, larger, more aromatic or with increased food and medicinal value.

As with other garden plants, herbs can be annuals or perennials. The annuals are grown from seed and will flower, if allowed to, and die down in one growing season, between spring and autumn; the perennials will grow from seed or small plants obtained from cuttings or division. Some of the perennials will also die down in autumn so that only the rootstock remains, but some are evergreen, and the leaves can be used all through the winter. Those that grow conveniently like this are: salad burnet, chervil, parsley, rosemary, thyme, sage, lavender, bay, hyssop and winter savory; some other herbs can be encouraged to go on producing top growth into early winter if covered with cloches, or through the winter if potted and brought indoors, such as chives, mints, lemon balm, pot marjoram and lemon verbena. Some of the shrubs may not survive a severe winter — for instance rosemary, sage, bay and hyssop, and if it looks like being prolonged and chilly, they must be protected from the cold as far as possible. A thick, wide-spreading mulch will help the roots, and enclosing the top growth in straw or conifer branches wrapped round with polythene, securely tied against wind, will keep the worst of the cold out. Leave a space at the top for a little air to penetrate and remove the wrappings as soon as it is safe to do so.

On the whole, about two thirds of the commonly grown herbs do die completely or to ground level, in autumn, and so for some at any rate, one must resort to preservation in order to use them between October and April. With modern methods, such as green drying, or deep freezing, the flavour and aroma can be retained almost *in toto*, and lack of fresh material need not be a deterrent to herb cookery, or any other uses to which they may be put. Most herb seeds are sown in spring in March or April, depending on the weather and the area. There can be a difference of four of five weeks between sowing dates, according to the air temperature and the rate at which the soil in your garden warms up, and it is much better to sow later than to rush the seeds into the ground, only to have them rot in cold, wet soil.

In any case, waterlogged soil cannot be broken down to the fine tilth required for seed sowing; it needs to be almost breadcrumb structure. Digging, knocking down the lumps with the back of the rake, and then repeatedly raking will gradually reduce it to the fine state in which seeds will germinate and the seedlings can establish and grow. Take out the weeds at the same time, particularly the roots of the perennial kinds, such as bindweed and couch grass; also remove debris such as stones, sticks, glass, pieces of clay pot, marbles, tin cans, and all the other clutter that is likely to be found in the average garden soil.

In the border or vegetable garden, herb seeds are most conveniently grown if the seeds are sown in rows or drills, as vegetables are, drawing out a shallow drill ¼–½ in. deep depending on the size of the seed. As the seedlings will, in most cases, need thinning later, it pays to sow the seeds sparingly in the first place. Choose a calm day, when the soil is nicely moist, give it a final rake down, and cover the seed thinly. If the soil structure is not good, germination can be encouraged by lining the drills with one of the soilless seed composts, suitably moistened.

Some herbs are grown from rooted cuttings, particularly the shrubby ones, and these are taken generally in summer, using soft tip or semi-ripe shoots. The majority which are propagated in this way root easily and it does not take long to increase or replace one's stock. The tip cuttings, about 3 in. long are put round the edges of 3-in. pots, in one of the proprietary cuttings composts, covered with a polythene bag secured with a rubber band, and put in a warm shady place until they begin to lengthen. When this happens, they have rooted, and may be potted on separately. Semi-ripe cuttings 5 or 6 in. long are taken later in the summer and need only be put, in their pots, in a cold frame or under a cloche out of doors. They will take longer to root and are usually best planted out in the spring following rooting.

Some herbs can also be propagated by division in spring or autumn, as herbaceous perennials are.

Whatever method of increase is chosen, once the young plants have settled down and are growing well, the routine cultivation through the season need only consist of thinning the seedlings, hoeing or hand weeding, watering when the weather is very dry, and perhaps giving the occasional liquid feed. Don't overdo the feeding, however; in many soils it will not be necessary, and too much tends to make herbs less aromatic and less well flavoured. They become soft and leafy, and it is the more hard grown kinds that contain the most in the way of essential oils, nutrients and minerals.

Where the appearance of the herbs is important, for instance in a herb garden or border, or when they are grown mixed with other plants, some will need trimming and cutting back, to keep them tidy. They can look very straggly when they have finished flowering, and get blown about and flattened by the wind. The small shrubby herbs tend to get unkempt unless sheared back occasionally.

Fortunately troubles such as insect pests and fungus diseases are few and far between as far as herbs are concerned; it has been said that they carry their own built-in resistance to such invasions, which is perhaps why they have such considerable medicinal values. Such pests and diseases as they do get are specific to the herb concerned and will be mentioned in the individual description in the alphabetical list, together with the remedy.

Container grown herbs

Two points are particularly important for growing herbs in this way: good compost, and good light. As with any pot or box grown plant, good compost is essential, that is, one which is well drained, and to which not only has plant food been added but in the right proportions. The John Innes compost No 1, is very suitable containing, as it does, 7 parts by bulk good loam, 3 parts peat and 2 parts coarse sand, together with 4 oz of the J.I. base fertiliser and ¾ oz chalk, to each bushel of the mixture. No 2 and No 3 have twice as much and three times as much respectively of the base fertiliser and chalk. These composts can be bought ready made up, from chain stores and garden shops.

Sunlight is most important, so herbs should be put in a sunny position if possible, otherwise in the best light there is, whether outside on a windowsill or balcony, or indoors on a window ledge. If out of doors, try to find somewhere that is not plagued by wind and if inside, give them even temperatures and a humid atmosphere as far as possible.

Herbs seem to do best if grown in the larger containers, such as window boxes, troughs, and shallow tubs. They can also be grown in pots; the 4-in. size is the smallest that can be satisfactorily used for the majority of herbs. When planting in clay pots, put a little drainage material at the bottom of the pot, such as crocks (pieces of broken clay pot) with the curved side uppermost, and then fill in with compost to about half full. Sit the plant on top of this in the centre of the pot, and fill in with compost round it, firming it down with the fingers, and leaving ½ in. space at the top for watering; water in lightly to settle the plant into the compost. Re-potting, or potting on into larger pots, is usually done in spring.

Whatever else you do when watering container-grown herbs, don't give them a dribble every day. Give them a good watering which fills the space between the compost surface and the rim of the container, let any extra water drain through the drainage hole, and then leave the plant alone until the surface soil begins to dry; when this happens, it usually becomes lighter in colour. A dry pot is lighter in weight than a moist one and, if it is clay, it will produce a ringing tone when tapped with a wooden stick. The rule is: only water when the plant needs it as indicated by these signs, and not, for example, at 10.30 every Thursday morning, or every day as soon as the breakfast washing up is done. Herbs will probably die more quickly from overwatering than any other container-grown plant, so, if you must err, do so on the dry side. Remember, too, that in winter when they are virtually not growing, much less water is needed than in summer.

3
Herbs –
a Descriptive List

Angelica (*Angelica archangelica; Umbelliferae*)
Description A tall, stout plant 5–8 x 3 ft (2–3 x 1 metre), perennial if prevented from flowering, otherwise biennal. Large, dark green leaves divided into leaflets, and flat, spreading heads of creamy white flowers in July. Origin, Northern Hemisphere, introduced 1568.

Uses Young green stems and leaf stalks used for candying for cakes and dessert decoration, picked April-May. Leaves also sometimes used in cooking. Plant strongly flavoured in all its parts, reminiscent of juniper berries, said to be used in making the French liqueur Chartreuse. Roots recommended for medicinal use as a digestive and for blood cleansing.

History Said to be named after the Archangel Michael who brought the curative properties of the plant to the notice of a monk. It was once recommended for use against the Plague, and to ward off the evil eye, spells and wizardry in general.

Cultivation Put in small plants in spring and divide roots when established; seeds will distribute themselves in due course. If using seed, sow as soon as ripe in August, as viability lost very quickly, thin out when large enough to handle, or plant in permanent positions in autumn, about 1½ ft (45 cm) apart. Moist soil and semi-shady place preferred.

Balm, lemon (*Melissa officinalis; Labiatae*)
Description A hardy herbaceous perennial 2–3 x 1½ ft,
(60–100 x 45 cm), rather shrub-like in form Leaves are soft,
heart-shaped and wrinkled; whitish flowers are produced
June-August. Origin, Europe, naturalised in Britain; used
since the Middle Ages. Top growth dies to ground in winter,
but new shoots appear very early in spring.

Uses The strongly lemon scented leaves are used in drinks,
also in salads, sauces and omelettes. It is said to be useful for
indigestion and to relieve tension. A favourite plant for pot

Lemon Balm

pourri and perfumery, and is a plant liked by bees because the flowers contain much nectar.

History Used by the Greeks, melissa is the Greek word for honey bee. It was also used by the Romans, and in the days of the Tudors, leaves were strewn on the floors, and the oil was an ingredient of furniture polish. In the 18th century it was popular enough to warrant growing on a commercial scale in market gardens round London.

Cultivation Easily grown by division of established plants in autumn, or from seeds sown in spring in a frame. Germination takes 3–4 weeks, and young plants are put out early in September. Will grow in most soils and situations, but does best in sun and moist, well drained soil. Remove flowers to encourage leaf production.

Basil, sweet (*Ocimum basilicum, Labiatae*)
Description Half hardy annual, 2–3 x 1 ft (60–90 x 30 cm); light green, soft, hairy leaves up to 3 in. (7 cm) long; white flowers in August. Dwarf basil, a variety of this, grows to 6–9 in. (15–22 cm). Origin, tropical Asia, Africa and the Pacific Islands; introduced in 1548.

Uses Leaves strongly and sweetly aromatic, similar to clove, used in cookery, particularly in Italy, and in India for curries. Because of its powerful flavour, sparing use should be made of it. The oil is used in perfume, and medicinally it is particularly of help in curing headaches and migraines.

History Has had a chequered history, being loved and hated almost equally. Culpeper (1616–54) said that: 'This is the herb which all authors are together by the ears about and rail at one another like lawyers'. Ocimum is from *okimon*, a name used for the plant in ancient Greece; basilicum is from the Latin *basilica*, princely or royal.

Cultivation Sow seed in 55–60°F (13–16°C) in March; germination will take about a fortnight. Prick out, harden off and plant indoors in late May 9 in. (20 cm) apart, in sandy rich soil and a sunny position. Seedlings transplant badly, so either sow generously inside or sow outdoors in mid May, and thin later. Water freely in dry weather; pinch out the tops for bushiness. Dwarf basil is best for pot cultivation. Lift in early September and pot up, for early winter use, cutting back the top growth hard.

Bay, sweet (*Laurus nobilis; Lauraceae*)
Description A large, evergreen shrub or tree, not hardy in severe cold; can form a tree 20 ft (6 metres) tall in southern England. Insignificant pale yellow flowers in May, followed by black berries in hot summers. Origin, southern Europe, possibly introduced 1548.

Sweet Basil

Uses Leaves strongly flavoured and much used in cooking, alone or as part of a bouquet garni. Berries and leaves much used formerly for medicinal purposes.

History Used to make wreaths in Roman times to honour poets, (hence the term poet laureate) generals, athletes and students, particularly medical students. Culpeper considered that it 'resisteth witchcraft very potently', and advised that 'the berries are very effectual against the sting of wasps and bees'. The diarist John Evelyn recommended its use against ague. For many years it was used with other evergreens for decorations at Christmas.

Cultivation Any soil and a sunny, sheltered place suit it.

Sweet Bay

Young plants are put in during autumn or spring; heel cuttings can be taken in April, or 3-4 in. (7-10 cm) half-ripe cuttings in August in a cold frame, in pots, potting-on as required. Plant out next autumn in nursery bed for two years. Clip trained plants twice in July and September. A good container plant as pyramid or standard.

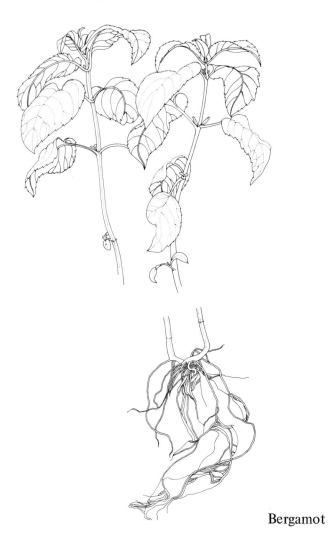

Bergamot

24

Bergamot (*Monarda didyma; Labiatae*)
Description A hardy perennial often grown in the herbaceous border, which dies down to the crown each autumn. Height 1-2 ft (30-60 cm), spread 1 ft (30 cm). Heads of tubular bright red flowers appear June-August. Origin, eastern America, introduced 1656. Also called Oswego Tea, or Bee Balm.

Uses The orange-scented leaves are mainly used for making tea, and on the Continent as a sleep-inducing tisane. They are also added to other drinks, chopped up for salads and occasionally used in pot pourri.

History Named after Nicolas Monardez, a Spanish botanist of the 16th century. Used by American colonists as a substitute for British tea during the time of the Boston Tea Party, and called Oswego tea after the American Indians from Lake Ontario who also used it for tea.

Cultivation Monarda prefers damp soil and does well at the waterside in sunny, open or semi-shady places. Plant in autumn or spring, mulch with compost each year at these times also. Cut back in autumn to tidy. Increase by dividing in spring.

Borage (*Borago officinalis; Boraginaceae*)
Description A hardy annual to 3 ft (90 cm) tall and 1½ ft (45 cm) wide, with large leaves to 9 in. (22 cm) long, rough and hairy, and brilliant blue flowers in drooping clusters from June to September. Origin uncertain – it may be a native plant, or it may be naturalised as a garden escape. It has been widely grown here in Britain, however, at least since Elizabethan times.

Uses The cucumber-like flavour that the fresh leaves and flowers give to drinks or salads is very refreshing; the flowers are used to give colour to pot pourri, or candied for cake decoration. It was once used medicinally for inflammations and redness of the eyes.

History It is possible that borage was introduced by the Crusaders; borage is said to be the herb of courage from the days of ancient Greece. Borage comes from the Latin *borra* meaning rough hair – the whole plant is bristly. It was considerably grown in the past as a salad plant.

Cultivation Sow seed outdoors in September or April, thinning to 12 in. (30 cm) apart in ordinary soil. Flowering will be in May, or June-July, depending on time of sowing. For winter cultivation indoors, sow seeds in containers in September. Flowering may continue through a mild winter.

Borage

Caraway (*Carum carvi; Umbelliferae*)
Description A taprooted, hardy biennial to 2 ft (60 cm) tall, with frond-like, much divided leaves, and umbels of small white flowers in the second June after sowing seed. Origin, Europe to India, cultivated in Britain for many centuries, possibly since the time of the Romans.

Uses The small, black, narrow seeds are the seed of the seedcake, or caraway cake; they are also used in biscuits, bread and cheese, in fact in very many dishes and recipes. Young roots can be used as a vegetable rather like parsnip or carrot, and the leaves in salads. Oil from the seeds is used to perfume brown Windsor soap, and some Continental liqueurs, for instance Kummel.

History Caraway was prescribed by Culpeper for flatulence, and the powder of the seeds put into a poultice would take away the 'Black and blue spots of blows and bruises'. It was described in an Egyptian papyrus in 2,500 B.C. and was also used medicinally by the Greeks and Romans. Seedcakes were popular in Tudor and Elizabethan days.

Cultivation Seeds are sown outdoors in spring in rows 1 ft (30 cm) apart, thinning to the same distance. Supply a well drained soil and sunny place – winter waterlogging will kill it. Harvest the seeds in July-August the following year.

Chamomile (*Anthemis nobilis; Compositae*)
Description Roman chamomile is a low growing herbaceous perennial 6-9 in. (15-22 cm) tall, spreading to about 1 ft (30 cm). Leaves very finely cut and fern-like forming a thick covering; white daisy flowers about 1 in. (2½ cm) wide from June-August. There is a non-flowering strain called the Treneague strain. It remains green through the winter. Origin: a native plant. There is also *Matricaria chamomilla*, wild chamomile, also a native plant, very similar in appearance, but taller, to about 15 in. (40 cm); this is an annual.

Uses Roman chamomile is used mainly for small lawns; it has some medicinal properties. Wild chamomile flowers are used considerably in medicine, and for shampoos. A tisane made of the flowers helps in digestion popular on the Continent, and a concentrated infusion acts as an emetic. All parts of the plant are strongly aromatic.

History Roman chamomile has been used for hundreds of years to make lawns; it was probably used for the lawn on which Drake was playing bowls when the Armada hove in sight. A chamomile of some kind is said to have been used by the ancient Egyptians, and it was certainly much used by the Greeks and Romans.

Cultivation Roman chamomile can be grown from rooted cuttings put out in spring in a sandy soil and sunny place about 6 in. (15 cm) apart for a lawn, or about 12 in. (30 cm) apart, if grown as a herb. Chamomile lawns are cut three or four times a year. Seed is sown in spring outdoors and later thinned, or indoors under glass in February.

Chervil (*Anthriscus cerefolium; Umbelliferae*)
Description A hardy biennial usually grown as an annual with delicate much cut and lacy leaves, flowering stems to 1½ ft (45 cm) and small white flowers in clusters from June to August in the second year from sowing. Origin, south-eastern Europe naturalised in some places.

Uses Leaves have slightly peppery and parsley-like flavour and are the part used, mainly for cooking, in sauces, soup and salads and in particular in omelette fines herbes. Chervil has a medicinal value in cleansing the blood and clearing skin troubles.

History Introduced by the Romans to this country, it continued to be used from Anglo-Saxon times continuously till late in the last century. Though little used now in this country, it is still very much part of modern French cooking. First used medicinally, and being considered an essential member of the herb garden in Elizabeth 1st's day, the flavour

28

was later found to be palatable, and it became popular for cooking.

Cultivation Sow seed outdoors in succession at four-week intervals from February to October in a well drained soil, in drills, thinning to 1 ft (30 cm) apart. It does not like drying out. Cut the leaves about 6–8 weeks after sowing, and a further crop will be produced. An August sowing will give leaves in September–October and early spring, or earlier if protected by cloches. Window boxes and pots are also suitable for overwintering. The seed loses its viability quickly.

Chervil

Chives (*Allium schoenoprasum; Alliaceae*)

Description Perennial bulbous plants with tubular, grasslike leaves to 4—10 in. (10—25 cm), which die down to ground level in late autumn. Round heads of purple flowers in June-July. There is a giant variety, to 1½ ft (45 cm) tall, much less well-flavoured. Origin, the Northern Hemisphere but rarely found naturally in Britain.

Uses Almost exclusively in cooking, for the delicate onion flavour of the leaves. Seldom used medicinally, though they are said to have some slight good effect on digestion.

Chives

History The cultivation of chives dates back to their use in 3000 B.C. by the Chinese and they have been used ever since by various civilisations. Introduced to this country by the Romans, the word schoenoprasum gives the plant its other, ancient common name of rush leek, since *schoenos* is a rush and *prason*, a leek, both being derived from Greek.

Cultivation Sow seeds outdoors in spring 10 in. (25 cm) apart in drills in medium to heavy soil and sun or shade; thin to clumps about 6 in. (15 cm) apart. Also increase by dividing in spring or autumn. Remove the flowers to encourage leaf production; water well in dry weather. Mulch in autumn with garden compost. Cover with cloches to protect from frost as long as possible, or pot up and grow in an indoor window sill in 6-in. (15-cm) pots.

Coriander (*Coriandrum sativum; Umbelliferae*)
Description A hardy annual 18 x 8 in. (45 x 20 cm) with delicate deeply cut, stem leaves; the base leaves are more solidly lobed. Both types have a very unpleasant strong smell. Tiny white flowers, tinted violet, are produced in flat heads in June–July. The round seeds are ripe in August. Origin: southern Europe, naturalised in Britain.

Uses The seeds are the part which is used most; they have a strong and unpleasant odour when unripe, but the disappearance of this indicates their ripeness; in fact their fragrance improves with age. The flavour is a mixture of lemon and sage. Powder of the seeds is much used in cooking, for instance curry, drinks including liqueurs and in both meat and dessert dishes of Spain, Greece, the Middle East and India.

History The name coriandrum comes from the Greek *koris*, meaning a bug, since the general odour was thought to be the same as that of bedbugs! Coriander seeds have been used at least since Egyptian times 1,000 years before Pliny; they are mentioned in the Bible, and there is record of their use here since 1289.

Cultivation Sow the seeds out of doors in April, preferably in a warm soil, otherwise germination is slow, in rows about 1 ft (30 cm) apart, thinning to 8–9 in. (20–23 cm). Also in September, or under glass in March, to plant out in May. Collect the seeds in August when their unpleasant smell has gone.

Dill (*Anethum graveolens; Umbelliferae*)
Description A hardy annual 2–3 x 1 ft (60–90 x 30 cm), rather like fennel to look at, with ferny, very finely divided leaves, and a stout stem; small dull yellow flowers come in large clusters between June and August. Origin, the Mediterranean countries; has been grown in Britain since the Roman occupation.

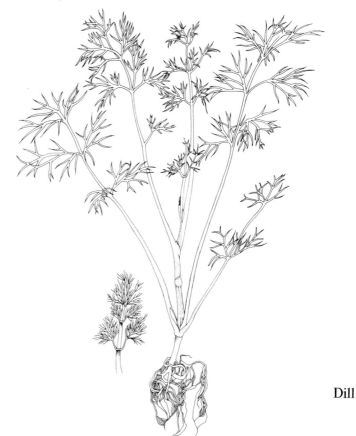

Dill

A simplified herb garden suitable for smaller gardens

A herb garden in the grand tradition

Uses Mostly culinary, in the case of the leaves, for salads, fish and vegetables; the seeds have a bitter taste but supply gripe water and are otherwise useful for digestion. The seeds are also mildly sleep inducing.

History The name comes from the old Norse word *dilla*, meaning to lull, because it was found to be effective in overcoming insomnia, and for soothing and calming generally. The ancient Egyptians used it, the Romans used it in Italy, and Culpeper in the 17th century remarked that 'It stayeth the hiccough'.

Cultivation Sow seeds outdoors in March-April in a moist but draining soil, in sun. Germination takes 14–21 days depending on the soil temperature. Rows should be about 1 ft (30 cm) apart; thin to 9 in. (22 cm). It does not like being transplanted. Sow also in July for an autumn supply. Keep well watered to prevent premature flowering. Self sown plants will be stronger than their parents.

Fennel (*Foeniculum vulgare; Umbelliferae*)
Description A tall, stout hardy perennial 5–8 ft (150–200 cm) tall by about 2 ft (60 cm) with a long white carrot-like root, rather short lived. Very finely cut, fern-like leaves, branching stems, and flat-headed clusters of yellow flowers in late summer. The variety *dulce* or *azoricum* is Florence fennel or finocchio, with a bulbous rootstock. A native of southern Europe, naturalised in Britain for many centuries, particularly near southern coasts and estuaries.

Uses The leaves have a strong and unusual flavour, and are used in cooking, mostly with fish. The basal stems of Florence fennel are eaten as a vegetable. Medicinally it was thought to have weight reducing properties; the liquid is used to make a solution for bathing the eyes. It can also be used as part of a face pack.

History Another herb dating back to Pliny's day, 2,000 years ago, and beyond to the Egyptian civilisations. It is mentioned in the Anglo-Saxon poem *Piers Plowman*, the reference there obviously being to its property of preventing the feeling of hunger. Florence fennel was first grown here in 1623.

Cultivation Sow seed outdoors in April in sun or slight shade and a moist, chalky soil, in rows 1½ ft (45 cm) apart, thinning to 1½–2 ft (45–60 cm) and stake the plant as it grows. Finnoccio needs a good warm summer, plenty of moisture and a rich soil; the base of the stem should be

Fennel

earthed up as it begins to swell so as to blanch it. For winter use, transplant into pots and keep indoors or under glass.

Garlic (*Allium sativum; Alliaceae*)

Description A hardy perennial usually grown as an annual in Britain, with a bulbous base made of separate segments called cloves, and grass-like leaves about 1 ft (30 cm) tall. Flower stem to 2 ft (60 cm), and flower white, appearing in summer. Origin doubtful, possibly the Kirghiz desert of Central Asia,

Garlic

but now grows naturally throughout the world including Britain.

Uses Has very strong flavour and odour, mostly onion-like, but with a characteristic all its own; this makes it a herb to use sparingly in cooking, where it has widespread use. Thought to have considerable antiseptic and antibiotic qualities particulary for stomach infections and blood cleansing.

History The word garlic is a compound one, from *gar*, a spear and *leac*, a leek. The derivation is Anglo-Saxon, but it is more than likely that it was introduced here by the Romans. It is said to have been fed to the slaves who built the Egyptian pyramids, and it has been used consistently in Britain for many centuries. In mediaeval times it was held to be an ingredient of medicines to cure leprosy.

Cultivation Plant the cloves in mid February, March or between September and early November, in a light rich soil and sunny place. Distance apart about 8 in. (20 cm), just below the soil surface, in rows 1 ft (30 cm) apart. Remove the flowering stems. Harvest when the leaves are yellow and hang to dry in a warm but shady place. Use a new site every year to avoid attack by white rot.

Horseradish (*Armoracia rusticana; Cruciferae*)
Description A stout perennial to 2 ft (60 cm) tall, with large basal leaves 1−2 ft (30−60 cm) long and small white flowers in May. The roots are fleshy and fanged. Origin, eastern Europe, naturalised in Britain, and sometimes a pernicious weed.

Uses Now mainly used in cooking, the peppery roots being grated, and used for horseradish sauce in particular. Also antibiotic qualities and much good effect on digestion. Was formerly prescribed against scurvy.

History Widely used for many centuries, particularly in Germany where it seems to have replaced mustard in the past. Its use in this country did not become general, however, until the 17th century, when ale was made from it. Horseradish has been placed in a variety of genera, and was once *Cochlearia armoracia; cochlea* is the Latin for spoon, in reference to the spoon shaped leaves of some species.

Cultivation Supply a rich, moist soil worked to 2 ft (60 cm) depth. Plant 3-in. (7 cm) root cuttings in March 1 ft (30 cm) apart, just covered with soil, in a bed separate from other plants. Lift all the plants in late autumn, store the larger roots in sand for cooking, and retain the smaller, also in sand, for planting next spring. Regular new plantings thus ensure the best quality roots for cooking.

Horseradish

Hyssop

Hyssop (*Hyssopus officinalis; Labiatae*)
Description A shrub-like, hardy perennial, semi-evergreen, to
1½ ft (45 cm) x 1 ft (30 cm) wide. Pink, white or blue-violet
flowers in July. Leaves narrow, like rosemary, but much less
leathery. Origin, Mediterranean area and east to Central Asia,
date of introduction to Britain not definite.

Uses The aromatic leaves have a mint-like odour, and are
slightly bitter and peppery, so use in cooking should be

sparing. Hyssop is used in Chartreuse liqueur. Medicinally hyssop tea has some use for catarrh and for clearing up bruises, and a further use is in perfume, especially eau-de-cologne.

History Thought to have been brought to Britain by the Romans, it was one of the herbs in a list made out by the Abbot of Cirencester in the 12th century; it is in some old Saxon manuscripts. Edgings to Elizabethan knot gardens were often of hyssop. Culpeper considered it 'an excellent medicine for the quinsy, or swelling in the throat'.

Cultivation Sow seed in April outdoors, thinning to 1 ft (30 cm) apart in rows 1½ ft (45 cm) apart. Take 2-in. (5-cm) cuttings in April-May in peat/sand, and put in a cold frame. Pot up when rooted and plant out in autumn. Bought-in plants are planted in autumn or spring. A heavy, wet soil and a cold winter are likely to kill it.

Lemon-scented verbena (*Lippia citriodora; Verbenaceae*)
Description A tender, shrubby plant, to 4 ft (120 cm), although 10—15 ft (3—5 metres) in its native Chile. Hardy in the West country outdoors. Shining, long-pointed, narrow leaves with lilac flowers in fluffy clusters in August. Introduced 1784.

Uses Strongly lemon flavoured leaves used in cooking and for tea, much drunk in Spain. Helps to ease troubles in the respiratory tract, as well as being pleasantly flavoured. Also added to pot-pourri.

History Formerly known as *Aloysia citriodora*, it is often confused with vervain, *Verbena officinalis*, also called verbena. This is a totally different plant with a slightly bitter flavour, native to this country and considered a sacred plant by the Druids. The roots were recommended to be worn as a charm for use against scrofula, as late as 1837.

Cultivation Grow from tip cuttings taken in spring, rooted

under glass in warmth. Pot on as required and, after hardening off, plant out in late May—June in a sunny sheltered place, and dryish, rather poor soil. Mulch heavily for winter, or lift and pot up in autumn for indoor growth, cutting it back by about half.

Lovage (*Levisticum officinale; Umbelliferae*)
Description A perennial with stout, hollow stems to 6 ft (2 metres) tall; it has fleshy roots and toothed leaves divided into leaflets like celeriac. Tiny, greenish yellow flowers appear in clusters in July. Origin, the Mediterranean area; it may have been introduced by the Romans.

40

Lovage

Uses Strong celery aroma and flavour from entire plant the whole of which (except the roots) is used in cooking, especially for soups and casseroles, giving a yeast like flavour. Medicinal uses included relief of eye troubles, as a gargle and mouthwash, and as a deodorant, using the leaves in bath water.

History The common name is a corruption from *levisticum* by way of love-ache, its only name some centuries ago. The generic name itself is a corruption of *Ligisticum*, from Liguria, in Italy. It is reputed to have been of help in romantic troubles, and was grown regularly in herb gardens until the last century.

41

Cultivation Sow the seeds when ripe in late August-September as the period of viability is short, and transplant the following spring to 3 ft (1 metre) apart, in moist well drained soil. Mulch every year. Also increase from root cuttings, each with an eye, in spring, put 2 in. (5 cm) below soil level.

Golden Marjoram

Marjoram, sweet or knotted (*Origanum majorana; Labiatae*)
Description A half-hardy annual 8 in. (20 cm) tall, rather bushy, with small greyish green slightly hairy leaves, and round green 'knots' from which tiny pinkish flowers come from June onwards. Origin, North Africa, introduced 1573. *O. vulgare* is a native plant of chalk downland, commonly called Oregano.

Uses Sweet and unusual aroma to the leaves, which are much used, both fresh and dried in cooking; especially good for flavouring sausages. Also used in perfumery and has mild antiseptic qualities, due to the thymol content.

History It was used a great deal by the Greeks and may well have been introduced by the Romans though the official date is much later. Culpeper said that 'it is so well known that it is needless to give any description of it', so it must have been in every garden in the 17th century. Now much used in Italy.

Cultivation Sow seed outdoors in rows 12 in. (30 cm) apart, in mid May, earlier in warm sheltered gardens, and thin to 10 in. (25 cm) apart. Provide a sunny place, and fertile, medium soil. Seedlings are slow to grow; weeding is important. Good for pot cultivation, but pot marjoram (*O. onites*) will be needed for winter use. This is perennial, but less well flavoured. Trim hard back in late summer and pot up in autumn.

Mint (*Mentha* species; *Labiatae*)
Description Perennial, mostly hardy herbaceous plants, with wide-spreading roots, stems to 1–2 ft (30–60 cm), and rounded or pointed leaves. Inconspicuous purplish or white flowers in July-August. Species cultivated: *M. spicata*, common mint, spearmint; *M. rotundifolia*, apple mint, smelling of apples; *M. citrata* 'Eau de Cologne'; *M. rotundifolia variegata*, green and cream edged leaves; pineapple mint, will not survive winter cold and damp. *M. piperita*, pepper mint.; *M. aquatica*, water mint. Origin, Europe including Britain.

Uses Mainly culinary, the leaves having varying fragrances and flavours as above. Leaves contain menthol and are good for summer drinks, and *M. citrata* is said to be an ingredient of Chartreuse liqueur. *M. piperita* leaves make a good digestive tea, so also does *M. aquatica*. Pepper mint is much used also in confectionery.

History Used by the Greeks and Romans, mentioned in the Bible, and widely used in Britain since at least the 9th century, when it was included in the monastic list of herbs. It has always been popular in this country up to, and including, the present day. Chaucer mentioned it in a poem, and Culpeper said that 'Applied with salt, it helps the bites of mad dogs'.

Cultivation Plant between autumn and spring; propagate by

Mint

division at these seasons also, or lift rooted stems and plant these. Damp soil is preferred, but it grows so easily that it needs curbing rather than encouraging, except for pineapple mint, which is slow to grow and less vigorous. It is advisable to root cuttings of this and keep them in the greenhouse through the winter; all will grow well in containers. If rust infects the plants, (small red-brown spots on leaves and stems) destroy them and plant afresh in a different place.

Nettles (*Urtica* species; *Urticaceae*)
Description Hardy perennial and annual plants, which reach 1–5 ft (30–145 cm), having pointed toothed leaves and green flowers in summer. *U. urens* is annual, 1 ft (30 cm) and flowers all season; *U. dioica* is perennial; both are native, but *U. pilulifera* was introduced by the Romans and has flowers in rounded clusters. It is annual and grows to 2 ft (60 cm).

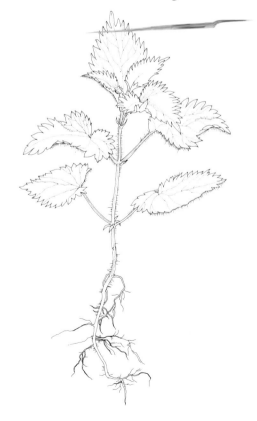

Nettles

45

Uses Leaves picked young are a substitute for spinach; they contain iron and silicic acid, and are good for cleaning the blood in spring. They are a good diuretic. The fibres were once used to make into a kind of linen, before cotton came into widespread use. The stinging feeling produced by the leaves is due to a substance similar to histamin and similar to the hormone secreted by the pancreas.

History The Roman nettle has the story attached to it that the Roman soldiers, having been told that the climate of England was bitterly cold, brought quantities of this species to rub on them, producing a warm tingling sensation. It was thought to represent envy in mediaeval flower symbolism, and Culpeper thought that 'seed being drunk was a remedy against hemlock, nightshade, mandrake or such herbs as stupify the senses'.

Cultivation, As it is such a well known weed, advice on this seems unnecessary.

Parsley (*Petroselinum crispum; Umbelliferae*)
Description A hardy biennial usually grown as an annual, to about 1 ft (30 cm) by 6 in. (15 cm) wide; it is thinly taprooted with very much cut and curled leaves, and tiny green-yellow flowers in flat-headed clusters from June to August. Origin, central and southern Europe; naturalised in Britain.

Uses Leaves strong and distinctive flavour, widely used in cooking. It contains an appreciable quantity of vitamin C, so has a useful nutritional quality, and stimulates the digestion. Parsley water is said to be good for encouraging the disappearance of freckles.

History Parsley was used daily in ancient Greece, and it seems likely that the Romans introduced it to Britain, though officially it arrived in 1548, being brought here from Sardinia. Its reputation for slow germination is said to be because it goes to the Devil seven times and back before

46

sprouting. The common name is a corruption of petroselinum, via *petersylinge* and *perseli.*

Cultivation Sow in March-April for a summer crop in moist
fertile soil and sun or shade; rows should be 1 ft (30 cm)
apart, with 6 in. (15 cm) in the row. A warm soil will speed
germination, which can take 10–28 days. For winter use, sow
in July, and protect in winter with cloches if snow is likely.
Remove flowerheads to encourage leaves. It is a good
container herb; for pots a 5-in. (12-cm) size is best.

Parsley

Rosemary (*Rosmarinus officinalis; Labiatae*)
Description, An evergreen shrub, hardy except in severe weather and wet soils, to about 4 ft (120 cm) in gardens by about 5 ft (145 cm). Very narrow, dark green leaves 1 in. (2½ cm) long, and pale purple flowers in May. Origin, southern Europe and Asia Minor, probably introduced in the Middle Ages.

Uses The leaves are pungently and pleasantly aromatic, giving a distinctive flavour in cooking; the oil contained in them is similar to eucalyptus. Rosemary is said to have an invigorating effect, and helps in restoring energy. It can also be used to improve the condition of skin and hair.

Rosemary

History The name comes from the Latin *ros* dew, and *maris* the sea — it grows naturally near the sea. Greek students twined it in their hair to help them think at examinations, and it was used in Greece at weddings, christenings and

48

Above: Tubs provide an ideal way of growing herbs in town gardens.

Above left: A small herb garden in a cartwheel, one of the traditional ways of growing herbs. *Above right:* A diamond made from old floor joists provides a simple, small area for growing herbs.

A simple herb garden can readily be constructed with seasoned wood

funerals. It was thought to be a disinfectant, even against the Plague.

Cultivation Plant in a sunny place and well-drained soil in spring; regular use will do all the pruning necessary. Easily increased from tip cuttings taken in March, putting four in a 4-in. (10 cm) pot in a frame or greehouse. Later cuttings in August are also possible.

Broad Leaved Sage

Sage (Salvia officinalis; Labiatae)
Description An evergreen shrub, hardy except in severe winters and damp soil. Height: 2 ft (60 cm) with the same spread. Grey-green, wrinkled, slightly woolly leaves, with

purple or white flowers in early summer. Origin, southern Europe and the Mediterranean area, introduced in 1597 or earlier.

Uses The strongly aromatic, slightly bitter leaves are much used in cooking, in particular with pork or duck. Sage tea is said to be good for gargling and as a mouth wash; it helps in the digestion, and in clearing a stuffy head if the steam from an infusion is inhaled.

History The name comes from the Latin *salveo*, to save or to heal, and it was considered by the Romans to be a veritable cure-all, and very much the most effective of all the medicinal herbs. An Arabic proverb says 'How can a man die who has sage in his garden?' The Greeks regarded it as a sacred herb, and it was even thought, during the 17th century, to delay the onset of symptoms of old age.

Cultivation Plant in spring in well-drained soil and a sunny place, in moderate fertility. A heavy wet soil is to be avoided. Easily grown from seed sown in late April, which takes about three weeks to germinate; also increased from 3-in. (8-cm) cuttings taken in August and put in a cold frame. Pot on singly and plant out the following spring.

Salad burnet (*Sanguisorba minor; Rosaceae*)
Description A decorative, hardy, herbaceous perennial, low growing, with flower stems to 1–1½ ft (30–45 cm). The toothed leaves are pinnate and nearly evergreen, and purple-tinted round heads of tiny green flowers come all summer. Origin, Europe; native to this country.

Uses Mainly for the leaves which are cucumber flavoured, and put in salads, soups and drinks. Used in the same way as borage. Also said to have value as a tonic.

History The name is derived from the latin *sanguis,* blood and *sorbere*, to soak up; there is a story that a Hungarian king gave orders for the juice of the plant to be used on the wounds of 15,000 of his soldiers after a battle. The Greeks

grew it, also for medical purposes. First deliberately cultivated in the 16th century in this country. Culpeper, in the
17th century, thought it had 'a drying and an astringent
quality . . . . . to staunch bleedings inward or outward'.

Cultivation, Easily grown, salad burnet prefers light soil. Sow
seed when ripe in summer, or the following spring, thinning
plants to 9 in. (23 cm) apart. Established plants can be
increased by division in early spring. It makes a good
container herb.

Savory (*Satureia* species; *Labiatae*)
Description *Satureja hortensis,* summer savory; an annual
plant to 8 in. (20 cm) with narrow leaves ½ in. (1 cm) long,
and pale lilac flowers in spikes from July-September. *S. montana,* winter savory; a hardy perennial, semi-evergreen,
subshrub to 15 in. (35 cm), otherwise similar to summer
savory. Origin, southern Europe, introduced around 1562, or
earlier.

Uses Leaves are strongly aromatic, nearer to a spice than a
herb, used in cooking, mainly to flavour beans, but also in
salads, soups and with fish; gather the leaves before the
flowers appear. The savories are good bee plants. The leaves
are sometimes used to help in digestion.

History Vinegar flavoured with savory was as much used by
the Romans as mint sauce is used by us. The word satureja is
thought to come from satyr, the plant being once considered
as an aphrodisiac. The leaves were said to alleviate the pain of
bee and wasp stings.

Cultivation Summer savory is grown from seed sown in April
in rows 1 ft (30 cm) apart, thinned to 6 in. (15 cm). The
leaves can be gathered twice, in August and in October, for
drying. Cover the seed lightly, otherwise germination is poor.
Winter savory can also be grown from seed, by division in
spring, or from 2-in. (5-cm) cuttings taken in May, put in a
frame, and then potted on and planted out the following
spring.

Sorrel, French or buckler-leaved (*Rumex scutatus; Polygonaceae*)
Description A hardy perennial, rather sprawling plant, dying down every autumn; height of flowering stems to 1 ft (30 cm), with a similar spread. Leaves are rounded shielded shaped, about 1½ in. (4 cm) wide, slightly fleshy; insignificant greenish flowers appear in summer. Origin, Europe, North Africa, West Asia; introduced but sometimes naturalised in this country.

Uses The rather bitter leaves are very good for soup, but otherwise should be used sparingly for flavouring as they are

Sorrel

very strong tasting. Also said to have diuretic qualities and to contain vitamin C.

History Culpeper said that the leaves of all the sorrels were of 'great use against scurvy if eaten in spring as salads'; the Greeks and Romans were convinced of their use in kidney troubles. Sorrels were a popular medical herb but parts of the plants contain oxalic acid, and the leaves should therefore be used sparingly.

Cultivation Plant in spring or early autumn in moist, slightly heavy soil allowing 1 ft (30 cm) between the plants; remove the flowering stems to encourage leaf production. Divide in spring or sow seed in April, thinning when large enough to handle.

Tansy (*Chrysanthemum* or *Tanacetum vulgare; Compositae*) **Description** A hardy herbaceous perennial to 2 ft (60 cm), with toothed leaves cut almost pinnately, up to 5 in. (12 cm) long, and small, flat, heads of yellow flowers from July-September. Origin, Europe, native to this country. There is a curled leaved form.

Uses The leaves are strongly aromatic, rather like camphor, and can be used in the same way that mint is with roast lamb; they have many other culinary uses. Tansy tea was used for colds and rheumatism, and a distillation of the leaves is said to be good for the complexion, removing freckles and sunburn.

History The common name comes from athanasia, or immortality, so it must originally have been thought to have much medicinal virtue. Tansy puddings were very popular in Elizabethan days, but might be considered very bitter now. However, an old recipe for this includes brandy and syrup of roses, so it is possible that it might be palatable!

Cultivation Easily grown, as would be expected of a native plant; any soil and situation will suit it. Division of the plant

in spring is the usual method of increase, putting each piece
1 ft (30 cm) apart. It needs controlling, otherwise spread is
rapid.

Tarragon (*Artemisia dracunculus: Compositae*)
Description An evergreen perennial, hardy unless the weather
is very cold or the soil badly drained, particularly in
winter; to 2 ft (60 cm) tall, spreading to 2 ft (60 cm) also.
Leaves narrow and linear, with insignificant greyish flowers.
The French variety is the best to grow because of its flavour.
Origin, southern Europe, introduced 1548.

Uses The leaves have an unusual and particularly pleasing

54

flavour, and are used to make tarragon vinegar and for all sorts of savoury dishes. Also for sauce tartare and Continental mustard.

History Although a very popular herb in culinary quarters, it has virtually no medical history; the common name is derived from the French *estragon*, a little dragon, − it was thought to be of use in healing the stings of venomous animals. In Tudor days, it was grown only in the Royal gardens.

Cultivation A well-drained, even dryish soil is essential, and preferably a sunny sheltered place, though an exposed site will do, if the soil is light. Plant in spring or September at 2 ft (60 cm) apart, and transplant about four years after the original planting, to maintain the flavour. Increase by division in spring. Seed does not set in this country. Protect in severe weather. Container cultivation is not easy, but the skilled gardener may like to pot up a few plants.

Thyme (*Thymus vulgaris; Labiatae*)
Description Common thyme is a hardy evergreen shrublet to 8 in. (20 cm) tall, spreading to 1 ft (30 cm) and more; tiny leaves, and lilac coloured flowers from June-August. *T x citriodorus* is similar but with broader, lemon-scented leaves. Origin, southern Europe, introduced before 1548.

Uses Considerable culinary use for the highly aromatic leaves, particularly with meat and savoury dishes generally, and in Benedictine liqueur, also lemon thyme in custard. The essential oil, thymol, is the part which helps coughs, and catarrh. Thyme is said to have considerable germicidal action. Also good for baths, and is used in toothpaste. Lemon thyme is used in perfumery.

History Extensively grown by the Greeks and Romans, it was probably brought to this country by the latter, who prescribed it as a cure for melancholy. The Greeks regarded it as an emblem for courage and an infusion was even recommended in 1633 for a cure for shyness. It has a considerable medical use today, so altogether it is essential to any herb garden.

Cultivation Easily grown by dividing in spring, or from 2-in long cuttings taken in early summer, put in a frame, potted on when rooted, and planted out in September. Seed is sown in spring (not lemon thyme) and treated in the same way, the final distance between plants being 1 ft (30 cm) either way. A sunny place and a light soil are preferred, preferably alkaline. It is a good container plant.

Thyme

4
Harvesting, Preserving and Storing Herbs

With a supply of herbs in your garden and the knowledge of how to harvest, preserve and store them, you can make sure of having the flavours you require for cooking throughout the year. What's more, you will be able to turn to your winter store for beauty aids and soothing drinks when fresh herbs are unobtainable. Preserving herbs is not difficult. There was a time when every housewife would know about such things. Drying is the most commonly used method and is very good, and those who own a home-freezer will find that many basic herbs can be 'put on ice' so to speak until they are needed.

Harvesting might sound a rather grandiose word if you have but a few herbs in pots on your window ledge, but it applies just as much to gathering in a few stems as it does to vast quantities. In any case, you must never pick or cut more herbs to be dried – or frozen – at any one time than can easily be dealt with.

Where the leaves are to be preserved cut just before the herb comes into flower. The reason for this is that much of the strength of the plant would go into the flowers and you wouldn't get such a tasty end-product. Left until after the flowers have faded you get the problem of what to do with the stems and seeds. If the worst comes to the worst and you return from a holiday to find the season more advanced than you expected and the herbs already in flower, you can still manage, even mixing flowers and leaves in together. This will not give a first-class result, either for colour or flavour, but would 'do'.

Herbs should not be cut on a wet day; choose a bright sunny one. Leave it until after the dew had disappeared so the foliage is dry, and pick before the sun gets very hot.

Using a sharp implement, where necessary, you can cut the stems of small-leaved plants to make life easier for drying and dealing with the herb later on. Large leaves can be picked individually but whatever you do, be careful not to damage them, especially such fragrant ones as lemon balm which suffer from bruising.

Marjoram and thyme are easy herbs to dry. When picking basil always keep some leaves on the plant as this seems to encourage others to grow. Be careful leaves do not darken. If drying in bunches, 2–3 sprigs per bunch, no more. Borage is not a simple herb to dry, nor is chervil. Chives are far better used fresh or frozen. Dill and fennel leaves can be dried but are best for their seeds. Parsley requires care, and should be picked before it bolts.

Plants from which the seeds are to be harvested should be left until the heads turn brown. You have to watch your timing carefully or the seeds will fall and scatter. Better be early than late. Pick on a dry day. Caraway, coriander, dill, fennel and lovage are good for their seeds.

Chamomile flowers are dried for making into teas, pot-pourri and so on. Other herbal flowers, such as tansy, can also be dried. Pick them on a dry day before they are fully opened.

Garlic is something of an exception as far as drying herbs is concerned. Harvest in the autumn. Leave it on top of the ground or in a warm, (not hot) dry atmosphere until ready, then store in a cool, airy place as you do onions.

Angelica stems for candying must be young and tender; get ready for that in April to May.

Herbs that are to be home-frozen should be picked when young and very fresh, and dealt with as quickly as possible.

Drying really means that the herbs need to be in a steady warm temperature with the dry air circulating all the time to take away moisture, and there should be no risk of condensation. Drying in the sun, which might sound tempting, is not always effective and can mar the colour. Generally, the more quickly herbs are dried the more of their aroma is preserved.

Most homes have plenty of suitable spots. An attic which is warmed by the sun, that is clean and airy and which doesn't suffer from quick heat loss at night; a spare room; an airing cupboard; the cooker; the kitchen: a garage which is not likely to be filled with petrol fumes, can all be used successfully; always avoid placing herbs in the sun's rays.

You can tie herbs, keeping each variety to itself, in bunches and hang them up to dry. Keep bundles small. They could become mildewed in the middle if too full. When there is a danger of them becoming dusty, cover them with fine muslin. You know the herbs are clean to start with; if not you will have to wash them first, then leave them in the open-air to dry again.

Bunches take between 14–21 days to get crisp and brittle, at which stage they are ready to be prepared for storing.

An alternative method is to have drying trays ready. These can be wooden frames with a fine mesh base, or home-made from cake trays or roasting tins, over which butter muslin is stretched. Lay the leaves or sprigs a little way from each other. You can layer trays in an airing cupboard, as long as you know there won't be any damp clothes put in, too, and by leaving a gap between each layer the air can move freely.

Laying herbs in bunches or hanging them in a very cool oven can be both successful and speedy. The temperature should be as low as possible; if necessary keep the door ajar. If you can't get the temperature low leave the trays outside the oven with the door open, or hang herbs above the cooker. As soon as the herbs are ready, let them cool before storing.

Parsley is not an easy herb to dry, you have to be watchful with it, but is easy to freeze.

There are various schools of thought about the best way of coping with parsley, and it is by trial and error you arrive at the method that you like best. The secret is to keep colour and flavour successfully. There are those who maintain it must be plunged into boiling water in which a pinch of bicarbonate of soda has been added before it is dried. Others prefer it absolutely dry, and yet others who insist on plunging it into boiling water for a few seconds to make sure no insects are lurking inside the foliage.

You can hang one or two bunches of parsley in a hot oven, 400°F, Mark 6, for up to one minute, then reduce heat to lowest possible setting (below a quarter on gas cooker) and leave the oven door ajar until the parsley is brittle. If you do this make sure the parsley does not scorch.

Or you can hang it, or lay it on trays, in the oven at 225°F, Mark ¼, for about an hour and then leave it in a very cool oven until it is crisp.

Another way is to leave it on trays outside the oven with the temperature at 250°–275°F, Mark ½–1, until it is ready.

All of these methods work.

Seeds have to be looked after, too. Cut the tops off the plants with the seed heads attached and lay them carefully on prepared trays, then cover with clean, dry pieces of linen or cotton and leave in a warm, airy room until the seeds loosen. Beat out the seeds with a stick and lay them to dry in an evenly warm spot where the temperature must not go above 70°F. Turn them over daily. When fully dry they can be stored.

If you want to retain the natural cream colour of chamomile flowers — which is delightful — pick them when they are dry and lay them in a warm place, on trays, and turn them daily to prevent them lumping together.

Candying is another way of preserving, and for this flowers are usually chosen, but perhaps angelica is one of the best known of all, and for this you use the young, tender stems. To crystallise your angelica takes about two weeks, but if you do some for gifts as well, you will be making charming as well as more unusual presents for your friends.

Choose stems that are bright in colour and cut into 3-inch long pieces. Immerse in a boiling brine solution (¼-oz salt to 4-pts. water); leave to soak for 10 minutes, drain and rinse in cold water. Pop back into fresh boiling water, simmer until tender, 5–10 minutes. Remove, drain and scrape away outer skin.

Weigh the stems. For every pound allow 6-oz. sugar and ½-pint water. Dissolve sugar in the water, bring to boiling point, pour over stems. If there isn't sufficient syrup make more in the same way. Leave 24 hours. Drain syrup off, add 2-oz. more sugar to it, bring to boil, pour over stems, leave 24 hours. Repeat this process daily until the 8th day. On the 8th day add 3-oz. sugar and the stems to the syrup, boil for 3–4 minutes, return to bowl and leave 48 hours. On the 10th day repeat this process, by which time the syrup should be the consistency of honey when cold. Leave 4 days, Dry off in a cool oven, 100°F–120°F, or less than Mark ¼ with the door ajar.

When it is cold, store the angelica between layers of waxed paper in a clean, air-tight container.

Before you get around to storing herbs you must make sure you have an adequate supply of containers. Small glass jars with tight-fitting lids or corks are ideal, and these must be spotlessly clean and dry.

If you intend to keep herbs on the sprig, (sage, thyme, rosemary are excellent for this and useful for making bunches of herbs, or for putting into vinegars or oils as decoration) you do need suitably-sized jars.

You do for bay too, if you want to keep that on the stalk and pick leaves off as required. Bay leaves have a tendency to curl up at the edges. Should you be fussy, you can lay them, once they are dry, under a board, for about 10 days, to flatten. Bay leaves can be stored crumbled, whole or crushed. Whole is probably more useful as you can always break off as much as you want at any one time.

Removing leaves from herb sprigs once they are brittle is very easy. So large or small leaves can be crumbled or crushed, whichever way you prefer. Crumbled preserves the flavour longer, crushed and then powdered is easier for quick seasonings. To powder, roll crumbled leaves with a rolling pin and then rub through a fine hair sieve. Jar immediately.

There is a measure of insurance attached to using glass jars. It is easy to see if moisture appears in them. Should this happen, the contents could not have been dried sufficiently, so tip them out on to greaseproof paper or muslin and dry again.

Store the jars in a dark, cool place, or wrap dark blue paper round them, or use opaque jars. Label them clearly with the name of the herb and the date on which it was packed.

Dried herbs and seeds should be effective for up to one year. Some last better than others, though. Rosemary, sage, marjoram and basil, for instance, can be used for longer, whereas tarragon and lemon balm can begin to lose something of their flavouring after about nine months.

Seeds are best stored whole and crushed (or powdered) immediately before use.

There are various ways you can home-freeze herbs; to a certain extent it depends on how you want to use them. Whichever your method, wash, dry and freeze as quickly as possible.

One way is to snip chives with scissors, or chop mint, or borage or parsley, or whatever herb you want, lay it in ice cube trays, cover with cold water and freeze. Remove the cubes, wrap each one separately and bag or box together in herbs of one kind. Label clearly and date.

These cubes served in drinks, (see recipes) are often time-saving, apart from being decorative. You can add ice cubes straight into your sauces and casseroles.

Another way is to lay sprigs or leaves out on foil in the fast-freeze section and bag or box when frozen, making sure that all the air is expelled. Or, you can place the washed, dried herbs straight into containers, again making sure the air is all out, and freeze. Parsley frozen on the sprig crumbles immediately when rubbed in your fingers.

Frozen herbs will keep successfully for up to six months.

Thawed sprigs are not recommended for garnish. They can look rather limp and sorry for themselves.

Dried or frozen herbs are always worth preserving.

5
Cooking with Herbs

Growing your own herbs provides you with a splendid opportunity to be adventurous in your cooking. You can blend different flavours in stews and casseroles, create exciting sauces for fish, meat and pasta dishes, add interest to salads, to egg and cheese recipes, and make puddings and cakes, biscuits and breads that will be the envy of all your friends.

With herbs you can garnish and decorate to provide eye-appeal to your culinary creations and it is important that a dish looks as good as it tastes.

Certain herbs have become associated with different foods. Be guided, but not dominated, by this association. You have to experiment for yourself. Start with small quantities, as over-flavouring is unsatisfactory. A herb should complement and blend into a recipe, not be an overpowering element in it; and the amount that suits one person might not please another. So using 'a pinch', that is a quarter of a level teaspoonful, makes sense as a beginning.

You will also have to adjust the quantities according to whether you are using freshly picked. dried or frozen herbs, and realise that some are far more strongly flavoured than others.

Generally speaking, dried have a more concentrated flavour than fresh herbs, so use less; frozen ones don't have quite such a pronounced taste as those taken straight from the garden, so you might have to use more.

Parsley, mint, lemon thyme can be used without too much thought; chives too, if you like a slightly oniony touch.

Chervil, tarragon, thyme, bay leaves, savory, lovage, marjoram and hyssop have strong flavours and should be used sparingly.

Among well-known cookery terms that can bemuse inexperienced cooks are 'a bunch of herbs', 'a bouquet garni', 'aux fines herbes' and 'mixed herbs'. These terms can also stifle your imagination and ingenuity if you believe they are unalterable.

A bunch of herbs is not really any different from a bouquet garni. You make a bunch of herbs when you tie small sprigs of herbs with cotton or string to the handle of the pan and allow them to cook with other ingredients. They can easily be removed before dishing up. The sprigs recommended are parsley and thyme and a bay leaf. A bouquet garni can be exactly the same, or it can be thyme, parsley and bay leaf put in a muslin bag with three or four peppercorns.

The important thing is that you can make your own mixtures; rosemary, savory, marjoram, chervil, basil are all very suitable. Make the most of whatever you have available.

When a recipe calls for 'aux fines herbes', and this is usually for an egg or salad dish or a sauce, it generally means equal quantities of finely chopped chervil, parsley, tarragon and chives. But 'fines herbes' can also be a combination of three or more perfumed herbs, so you can take your pick.

'Mixed herbs' generally refers to thyme, marjoram, parsley and savory.

Make the most of herbs for salads. The fresh foliage, finely chopped, can make an amazing difference and flowers of bergamot or borage add colour as well. You can also make excellent dressings that are your own, exclusive 'blend'. For instance, add a handful of chopped mixed herbs, such as chives, tarragon, chervil or salad burnet, to a standard salad cream, mayonnaise or vinegar about 30 minutes before it is to be used. Add finely chopped, mixed herbs to soured cream or natural yogurt, seasoning to taste, on another occasion.

You can make your own seasonings for stews and soups and so on, by blending dried, powdered herbs.

A Victorian aromatic seasoning is: 3 oz. each basil, marjoram and thyme, 2 oz each winter savory and pepper-corns, 1 oz each bay leaves, mace, nutmeg, cloves, ½ oz dried, grated lemon peel. Pound them all together, sieve finely and store. Adding 1 level teaspoon powdered garlic makes a stronger flavour still. Use in quantities as required.

A useful seasoning for egg and chicken recipes is: 1 level tablespoon each dried powdered summer savory, tarragon, chervil and basil.

Aromatic mixtures such as these are easy to make, so never attempt to store one for too long; the flavour can deteriorate. The use of sauces in cooking is invaluable. Here in Britain, we tend to be somewhat stereotyped with our use of herbs for them. Parsley sauce is perhaps the best known and very good it is too, especially with fish or broad beans. You get the best flavour from it if the parsley is chopped, (it must be dry, otherwise the sauce will become coloured) and added after the sauce is made. You can toss in as much as you like.

But chervil can be used as a change; indeed, chervil makes an easy substitute for parsley in any case.

Finely chopped fresh fennel leaves are another alternative to parsley. This sauce is delicious with fish.

When housewives were unable to rush down to the nearest supermarket they had to rely on flavourings that were easily available. As a result they used their garden 'store cupboard'.

Here are some examples that are well worth trying. Put one or two bay leaves with milk to warm, not boil, and then allow to cool. Make rice, sago puddings with this milk. It is very good for custards, as well. Treat lemon verbena in a similar fashion for a baked custard.

Keep a bay leaf in a jar or tin with caster sugar. The sugar will add flavour to puddings and cakes.

To an apple pie recipe that includes cinnamon, add half a teaspoon crushed coriander seeds. Another tasty pie idea is to sprinkle a few dill seeds in with apple slices for a pie or tart.

Rhubarb is quite sharp, even when sweetened, but if you cook it with a few pieces of young, tender angelica stems much of the tartness will disappear.

Try just a pinch of powdered coriander in a summer junket.

For cakes and breads and biscuits, add your own herb flavourings; for instance, sprinkle coriander or caraway seeds on top of a loaf or cake; add one teaspoon powdered rosemary to a standard biscuit mixture. Mix caraway seeds into a dough.

Indeed, making the most of herbs is almost an endless task. For example, add a little chopped chervil to batter when you are frying fish, or a pinch of dried thyme into the pancake mixture when they are for a savoury meal. Add a teaspoon of sage to the batter for a sausage toad-in-the-hole.

Plainly cooked white fish can be on the boring side, not though if you add fennel, lemon thyme and marjoram to the milk in which the fish is boiled. While on the subject of fish, tinned salmon or tuna, mixed with mayonnaise, sprinkled with dill seeds, served on cracker biscuits are easy canapés.

Lovage, which is quite powerfully flavoured, makes an ideal alternative for celery in soups and stews.

Bay is strongly flavoured, and to begin with only use ½ leaf per two people. Use it when boiling bacon for extra good flavour.

Now let us have a look at which herbs to use with what.

Beef:	Horseradish, basil, marjoram, thyme, rosemary.
Pork and Bacon:	Sage, basil, rosemary, chives, parsley, bay.
Lamb:	Rosemary, garlic, summer savory, dill, bay.
Veal:	Thyme, sage, rosemary, lemon verbena, lemon balm.
Stews:	Bay, dill, garlic, horseradish, marjoram, parsley, thyme, hyssop (use sparingly), lovage (sparingly), sage, rosemary, tarragon, chives, coriander seeds (and for curries).

Soups:	Basil, (especially for tomato or turtle) mint (especially for pea), parsley, thyme, bay, fennel (for fish). Nettles and sorrel make soups in their own right.
Poultry:	Parsley, sage, summer savory, tarragon, thyme, rosemary, fennel.
Fish:	Fennel, sage, parsley, basil, chives, chervil.
Eggs:	Chives, tarragon, chervil, marjoram, basil, parsley, salad burnet (especially for omelets).
Hard Cheeses:	Basil, thyme, chervil, sage.
Soft Cheeses:	Mint, dill, sage, basil, caraway, chives, garlic, parsley.
Salads:	Salad burnet, chives, borage, fennel, tarragon, chervil, thyme, lemon balm, garlic, sage, angelica leaves, dill foliage.
Pasta:	Basil, chervil, garlic, mint, parsley, thyme.
Cabbage:	Parsley, caraway, finely chopped borage – added just before serving.
Peas:	Summer savory, mint.
Carrots:	Summer savory, mint, basil, parsley.
Potatoes:	Mint, parsley, chives, garlic.
Spinach:	Mint.
Beans:	Summer savory, sage, parsley.
Tomatoes:	Basil, marjoram, chives, parsley, lemon balm.
Stuffings:	Parsley, sage, thyme (lemon thyme good with veal), chervil.
Sauces:	Bay, dill (for fish), fennel (for fish), garlic, mint, parsley, horseradish, chervil, angelica leaves (sweet sauce).
Teas and Vinegars:	As you wish, (tarragon famous for vinegar).
Breads, Cakes, Biscuits:	Caraway, coriander, rosemary, basil.
Desserts:	Mint, lemon verbena, bay, caraway, angelica, dill, tansy.

Jams and Jellies:	Lemon verbena, mint, parsley.
Cold Drinks and Cups:	Borage and flowers, mint, lemon balm, rosemary, salad burnet, lovage, bergamot and flowers.
Garnishes:	Parsley, mint, thyme, rosemary, lemon balm, basil, chervil, savory, borage flowers, bergamot flowers, angelica, chives.

It would be wrong to finish this chapter without particular reference to nettles, sorrel and garlic.

The young leaves of nettle and sorrel can be cooked and eaten as a vegetable (see recipes) in the same way as spinach; both, too, can be used for soups. Gather nettles, tops only, in the spring when they are especially tasty – wear rubber gloves when you do!

Garlic, which can be used in all savoury dishes and for salads has a strong taste and powerful aroma. It is best to ask if guests like it, or use very carefully; too much can be off-putting.

Recipes

Starters

RABBIT TERRINE
1 medium-sized onion, roughly chopped
1 medium-sized rabbit, cut into joints
3 tablesp melted lard
Bouquet garni
Cold water
¼ lb fat bacon pieces
Rabbit liver
2 Cox's Orange Pippin apples, peeled, cored and quartered
½ lb pork, minced
½ lb pork sausagemeat
1 teasp chopped marjoram
1 tablesp chopped parsley
4 tablesp white wine
Salt and pepper
¾ lb lean streaky *or* back bacon rashers, de-rinded

Gently fry onion and rabbit joints in melted lard for about 5 min, add bouquet garni and sufficient cold water to cover, bring to the boil, put lid on pan, reduce heat and simmer for 45 minutes. Remove rabbit and, when cool, take flesh from bones. Mince the bacon pieces, rabbit, rabbit liver and apples, mix together with all the other ingredients, except the bacon rashers. Line a terrine, mould, or fireproof dish with the bacon rashers, fill with the terrine mixture, cover with foil. Bake in a low oven 150°C, 300°F, Mark 2, for 1¼–1½ hours. Leave to get cold, turn out and serve.

12 helpings

PORKY TERRINE

1 lb pig's liver
½ lb belly of pork
4 oz fat bacon
1 oz lard
6 onions, finely chopped
4 oz cranberry jelly
1 oz cornflour
¼ teasp cayenne pepper, *or* to taste
¼ teasp black pepper
1 level teasp salt
1 rounded teasp chopped marjoram, less if dried
Grated rind of 1 small orange
2 cloves garlic, crushed
1 sherry glass dry red wine
3 tablesp sherry
3 bay leaves

Mince the liver, pork and bacon together. Melt the lard and fry the onions until softened, but not browned. To the onions add the minced meats, and cranberry jelly. Mix together in a basin the cornflour, cayenne pepper, black pepper, salt, marjoram, orange rind and crushed garlic, stir in the wine and sherry; mix thoroughly. Add this mixture to that already in the pan, and stir over a low heat for 5 min. Butter a shallow brown earthenware dish and place the mixture in it. Smooth the top with a damp knife, and lay the three bay leaves on top. Put the dish into a roasting tin containing water and bake at 180°C, 350°F, Mark 4, for 1–1¼ hours. Allow to get cold and serve straight from dish accompanied by hot buttered toast.

12 helpings

CHICKEN LIVER PÂTÉ

1 medium-sized onion, finely chopped
1 clove garlic, finely chopped
8 oz chicken livers
1 oz butter
1 teasp any herb that suits your fancy (lemon verbena, tarragon, mint, for example)
Salt and pepper
3 oz butter, creamed
1 dessertsp brandy
Clarified butter

Fry garlic and onion in butter until beginning to turn golden; add livers, herb, seasoning, fry for another 3 minutes. Cool, chop finely, sieve or blend, and work in the creamed butter. Add the brandy, put into a china pot and coat with clarified butter. Serve with hot buttered toast or crumpets.

4 helpings

CHEESE PÂTÉ

1 oz butter
1 oz plain flour
¼ pt milk
4 oz grated Cheddar cheese
1 level tablesp mayonnaise
3 gherkins, chopped
Salt and pepper
1 level dessertsp chopped chervil *or* chives *or* tarragon *or* lovage

Melt butter, cook flour for a minute, gradually add milk, bring to boil, stirring, cook for 2 minutes. Remove pan from heat, stir in cheese, then the other ingredients. Make sure the cheese melts. Turn into a china pot, cover and leave until chilled. Serve with hot buttered toast.

3 helpings

LANSDOWNE SOUP

2 peppercorns, crushed
1 small sprig parsley
A little fresh thyme
A little basil
½ pt milk
1 bay leaf
Small sprig rosemary
1 oz butter
1 lb onions, sliced thinly
1 oz flour
1½ pt white stock
(can be made with a chicken stock cube)
Salt and pepper
Chopped chives

Wash herbs, put with crushed peppercorns in the milk; warm gently, but do not allow to boil, then let milk cool; leave about 10 minutes, strain. Melt butter, add onions and cook over low heat until they are soft but not browned. Stir in flour, cook, stirring, for 2–3 min. Slowly add stock, bring to boil. Cook 2 min, add strained milk and re-heat but do not boil. Season to taste. Serve garnished with chives.

6 helpings

NETTLE POTTAGE

2 oz butter
2 oz oatmeal
2 pt vegetable stock, milk *or* water
Salt and pepper
5–6 heaped tablesp finely-chopped young nettles

Melt butter in pan and fry the oatmeal until crisp and browned. Add the stock, bring to the boil, stirring. Sprinkle in seasoning, toss in the nettles, return to the boil, reduce heat, cover pan and simmer for 10–15 minutes.

4 helpings

72

SORREL SOUP
2 oz butter
2 medium-sized onions, finely chopped
6−8 oz fresh sorrel leaves, finely chopped
2 pt white stock
Salt and black pepper
12 oz potatoes, peeled and sliced thinly
2 tablesp cream
1 rounded tablesp chopped chervil

Melt butter, fry onions until tender, add sorrel, stock and seasoning. Simmer 10 minutes, add potatoes; cook 30 minutes, sieve or blend, re-heat, stir in cream. Serve garnished with chervil. If the soup is served cold, swirl the cream in it just before serving.

4 helpings

MINTED SUMMER SOUP
1 large cucumber, peeled and chopped
2 x 5-oz cartons natural yogurt
5−6 sprigs fresh mint
Seasoning to taste
Mint leaves for garnish

Put cucumber, yogurt and mint sprigs in blender, blend until smooth. Add seasoning, cover bowl and leave in a cool place to chill. Serve garnished with mint leaves.

4 helpings

TOMATO JUICE COCKTAIL
Fresh or canned tomato juice
Finely-chopped chervil *or* basil *or* parsley (can be put through blender)

Mix herb with juice, stir and leave to blend flavours for at least 30 min. Serve at room temperature, or chilled, garnished with leaves or sprigs of the herb chosen.

LENTEN CHAMP
1 lb potatoes, peeled and quartered
8 oz young nettle tops, chopped
Salt and pepper
Butter

Boil potatoes until tender, drain and mash. Wash nettles, cook in very little water until tender, drain and chop. Mix potatoes and nettles, season to taste. Serve in portions. Champ is eaten by making a well in each portion, putting butter in the hole, and dipping each spoonful of vegetable into the butter before eating. Chives can replace nettles if preferred.

4 helpings

Fish Dishes

SHRIMPS CRÉOLE
8 oz frozen shrimps *or* fresh, peeled shrimps
1 oz butter
1 small onion, finely chopped
½ green pepper, seeded and finely chopped
1 oz butter
1 oz flour
1½ lb tomatoes, skinned and chopped
Juice of the tomatoes
1 tablesp finely chopped fresh thyme, rosemary and basil *or*
    ½ tablesp dried
Salt and black pepper
1 level dessertsp sugar
A little water if required

Allow shrimps to thaw, drain well. Melt butter in a deep pan, gently fry onion and green pepper until soft (about 7 min). Stir in flour, tomatoes, herbs, salt, pepper and sugar, and cook with lid on the pan, stirring occasionally, until tomatoes are soft (about 20 min); if sauce gets too thick, add water. Add the shrimps and simmer for 4 or 5 min until hot. Serve with boiled rice or mashed potatoes.

4 helpings

74

SKEWERED MACKEREL

4 smallish *or* 2 large mackerel
8 small pickled onions
8 rashers streaky bacon
8 button mushrooms
12 bay leaves
Salt and pepper
Juice of 1 lemon
1 level dessertsp chopped fresh fennel leaves *or* thyme
¼ pt oil

Clean fish. Remove heads and backbones. Cut small fish into about six slices, large ones into 12 slices. Thread fish on skewers alternating with onion, rolled bacon rashers, mushrooms and bay leaves. Mix seasoning, lemon juice and fennel into the oil. Marinade skewered ingredients in this mixture for one hour. Cook under a hot grill, turning occasionally.

4 helpings

BLUSHING HADDOCK

4 portions haddock fillet
Salt and black pepper
2 tablesp oil
1 lb tomatoes, skinned and chopped
1 small onion, finely chopped
1 teasp fresh chopped basil *or* ½ teasp dried basil
1 tablesp chopped parsley
2 oz fresh breadcrumbs
1 oz finely-grated Cheddar cheese

Put the fillets in a lightly-greased shallow dish. Season well. In a saucepan put the oil, tomatoes, onion and basil; cover and simmer for 10 min, stirring occasionally. Sprinkle parsley over the fish, pour over the sauce. Mix breadcrumbs and cheese together and cover top of dish. Bake in oven at 180°C, 350°F, Mark 4 for 30–40 minutes.

4 helpings

KILLYBEGS HERRINGS

3 medium-sized carrots, chopped
2 onions, chopped
1 clove garlic, chopped
1 dessertsp chopped parsley
Sprig of thyme
1 bay leaf
2 cloves
4 peppercorns
½ oz butter
Cold water
Salt and black pepper
12 small herrings, gutted
1 onion, cut in rings
1 teacup malt vinegar

Put the carrots, chopped onions, garlic, parsley, thyme, bay leaf, cloves, peppercorns and butter into a saucepan; just cover with water, add seasoning, bring to boil, reduce heat and simmer until vegetables are cooked. Meanwhile, cut heads from fish and clean them. Transfer vegetables and any juice to a fairly shallow fireproof dish. Lay fish over, top with onion rings, pour in vinegar and sufficient water to cover the ingredients. Cover dish with foil and bake just above centre of oven at 190°C, 375°F, Mark 5, for about 25 min, until the fish is tender. (If large fish is used, cooking time will be longer.) Remove from oven and leave to cool in liquid.

12 helpings as a starter
6 helpings as a main meal with salad

76

STEWED EELS

1½ lb eels, skinned and cut into 2-in pieces
1 small onion, chopped
A bunch of herbs (sprig parsley, thyme, tarragon, *or* to your taste)
8 peppercorns
A blade of mace
1 tablesp lemon juice
Salt and pepper
White stock *or* water
1 oz butter
1 oz flour
Stock from eels
¼ pt single cream *or* milk
1 tablesp chopped parsley

Put eels, onion, herbs, peppercorns, mace, lemon juice and seasoning into a saucepan, cover with stock or water, bring to boil and simmer 35–40 min, until eels are cooked. Remove fish and keep warm. Reserve ½ pt strained liquid in which it was cooked. Melt butter, add flour, cook 2 min, slowly stir in stock, cook until thickened. Take pan off heat, add cream, re-heat a little, adjust seasoning, mix in parsley and pour over eels.

4 helpings

'FISH 'N' FENNEL'

1½ lb fillets of whiting *or* fresh haddock *or* cod
Oil
4 oz butter
1–2 tablesp freshly-chopped fennel
Salt and pepper

Brush fillets with oil and grill in usual way until cooked. Melt butter, stir in fennel and seasoning, put fish on warmed platter, pour sauce over and serve.

4–5 helpings

ANNE'S PLAICE
1 lb plaice fillets, cut into pieces about 1½-in
Seasoned flour
3–4 oz butter
¼ pt single cream
About ½ pt milk
1 teasp chopped young coriander leaves *or* parsley
A pinch of dried thyme
Chopped parsley *or* chopped coriander leaves for garnish

Dip the fish in seasoned flour and fry in the butter for 5 min, using a heavy pan. Shake frequently. Slowly stir in the cream, add the herbs, and sufficient milk to make a smooth sauce. As soon as the sauce is cooked (2–3 min), turn into a warmed dish, garnish and serve.

4 helpings

COLD COD SUPPER
4 cod cutlets *or* steaks
3 tablesp olive oil
2 tablesp tarragon *or* cider vinegar
1 shake garlic salt
½ bay leaf, broken into pieces
½ teasp each finely-chopped parsley, basil, lemon balm (*or*
    any combination that appeals to you)
Paprika pepper for garnish

Place cod in a shallow bowl, thoroughly mix other ingredients together, pour over fish, cover and leave to marinade for at least 2 hours. Lay buttered greaseproof paper in base of steamer. Put drained cod over and steam for 10–15 min depending on thickness of the fish. Leave to cool. Serve garnished with paprika pepper, surrounded by salad.

4 helpings

FISH CAKES

8 oz cooked white fish, skin and bone removed, flaked
8 oz mashed potatoes
1 teasp chopped parsley
1 teasp chopped chervil
Salt and pepper
½ oz butter, melted
1 egg lightly beaten
Egg and browned breadcrumbs for coating
Fat for shallow frying
Parsley sprigs

Mix fish, potatoes, herbs, seasoning and melted butter together with sufficient beaten egg to bind mixture. Divide into eight portions, form into cakes, coat in egg and breadcrumbs and fry, turning once during cooking, until golden brown. Drain and serve garnished with sprigs of parsley.

4 helpings

Meat Dishes

ROSEMARY LAMB

Dripping
1 whole leg of lamb
2 cloves of garlic, cut into slivers
10–15 rosemary leaves
Salt and black pepper
1 sprig of rosemary

Pre-heat oven to 220°C, 425°F, Mark 7. Melt dripping in roasting tin. Cut small slits in the fat of the meat and insert slivers of seasoned garlic and rosemary leaves. Spoon the melted fat over and cook above the centre of the oven, allowing 20 min per lb, plus an extra 20 min. Roast vegetables in your usual way. Serve the leg of lamb garnished with a sprig of rosemary.

8–10 helpings

TOPSIDE DE LUXE

2 lb topside of beef
1 large onion, chopped
2 cloves
6 peppercorns
1 bay leaf
1 sprig each parsley, thyme, rosemary
¼ pt each olive oil and malt *or* tarragon vinegar
2 oz dripping
¼ pt stock

Put beef in a dish, cover with the onion, cloves, peppercorns and herbs. Pour oil and vinegar mixture over and leave to marinade for 3 hours, turning at least once. Remove from marinade and fry quickly in melted dripping until sealed on both sides. Transfer to ovenproof dish. Pour in juices from the pan, the stock and 3–4 tablesp strained marinade. Cover with lid or foil and bake in centre of oven at 180°C, 350°F, Mark 4, for 1½ hours or until meat is tender.

5–6 helpings

WISE MAN'S PORK

4 pork chops
2 tablesp olive oil
1 oz butter
1 Spanish onion, finely chopped
1 lb cooking apples, peeled, cored and sliced
1 teasp freshly-chopped sage *or* generous pinch dried sage
Salt and pepper to taste
Demerara sugar

Cook chops in your usual way. While chops are cooking, heat oil and butter in a pan, add onion, apples and sage, cover pan and cook slowly, stirring or shaking occasionally, until apples are soft and onions tender (10–15 min). Add seasoning and sugar to taste. Serve chops coated with the apple and onion mixture.

4 helpings

Herb gifts are increasingly popular (Courtesy of Culpeper of London Ltd.)

Herb teas have far subtler flavours than more traditional brews (glass teapot Courtesy of Harrods of Knightsbridge)

STEAK–IN–A–BED
3–4 oz butter
1 lb frying steak of your choice
1 heaped tablesp freshly-chopped herbs *or* ½ tablesp if dried
Salt and pepper
Large pkt frozen puff pastry
Beaten egg

Pre-heat oven to 230°C, 450°F, Mark 8. Melt 2 oz butter in a pan and brown steak on both sides. Remove from pan and leave to cool. Spread butter thickly over top of steak, sprinkle with salt and pepper and half the herbs. Roll out pastry thinly, cut into two equal-sized pieces, each slightly bigger than the steak. Lay the steak, butter side down, on one piece of pastry. Spread butter on other side of steak, then sprinkle with seasoning and herbs. Dampen edges of pastry, place other piece on top, seal edges well. Brush with beaten egg to glaze. Cook near top of oven until pastry is ready (20–25 min).

4 helpings

TARRAGON BRAISED LAMB
1 lean shoulder lamb *or* other joint weighing about 3 lb
Flour
2 oz dripping *or* lard
Salt and pepper
½ bottle white wine
2 cloves garlic, chopped
2 sprigs tarragon
1 tablesp capers
¼ pt single cream

Rub the flour over the meat. Melt the fat in a roasting tin in a hot oven and brown meat on all sides. Transfer meat to an ovenproof dish, lower oven temperature to 180°C, 350°F, Mark 4. Season meat well, add wine, one sprig of tarragon and the garlic, cover with foil or lid and bake for 1½ hours, then add the rest of the tarragon, capers and cream, cook for a further 30 min.

6 helpings

LAMB PROVENÇAL

2 lb stewing lamb, trimmed and cut into neat pieces
1½ lb potatoes, peeled and thinly sliced
1–2 cloves garlic, crushed
3 medium-sized onions, thinly sliced
4–5 tomatoes, skinned and sliced
1 dessertsp chopped mixed herbs (less if dried herbs used)
Salt and pepper
A little butter *or* lard
Water

Grease a deep casserole. Mix crushed garlic into the onions. Layer ingredients in the casserole, sprinkling herbs and seasoning between each and reserving sufficient potatoes to make a final layer. Before putting this top layer on, pour in water to come just over halfway up the dish. Put in the potatoes, arranged neatly, spread the butter over them, cover the casserole and cook in middle of oven at 180°C, 350°F, Mark 4 for 1¾ hours, remove lid and cook for a further 30 min to enable the top potatoes to brown.

4 helpings

CORNED BEEF HASH

½ pt white sauce (thickness to suit own taste)
1 tablesp grated horseradish
1 tablesp single cream, evaporated milk *or* top-of-the-milk
1 tablesp chopped parsely
8 oz corned beef, diced
2 oz grated cheese
Parsley sprigs for garnish
Mashed potatoes

Make sauce in usual way, stir in horseradish, cream, parsley, corned beef, allow meat to warm through. Make a ring of mashed potato in a fireproof dish, place hash in the middle, sprinkle grated cheese over and put into hot oven or under grill until cheese has melted and begun to bubble. Garnish with parsley sprigs.

3 helpings

Game and Poultry Dishes

PIGEON PIE
2 young pigeons, cut into joints
½ lb rump steak, cut into small cubes
1 dessertsp seasoned flour
4 oz mushrooms, roughly chopped
4 oz lean bacon, de-rinded and chopped
Stock *or* water
6 oz flaky pastry

For the forcemeat balls

2 rounded tablesp fresh breadcrumbs
1 tablesp melted dripping *or* lard
1 level dessertsp chopped parsley
½ teasp chopped lemon verbena, a pinch if dried
1 small egg, lightly beaten, *or* ½ large egg

Sprinkle seasoned flour over cubed meat and pigeon joints. Pre-heat oven to 220°C, 425°F. Mark 7. Make forcemeat balls: chop pigeon livers, and mix all the ingredients except the egg together, add sufficient egg to make a binding texture and form into small balls. Place half the bacon and mushrooms in the bottom of an ovenproof dish, with some of the forcemeat balls, cover with the pigeon joints and steak, sprinkle remaining bacon and mushrooms over. Fill up side gaps with the rest of the forcemeat balls. Half fill dish with cold stock or water. Cover with the pastry, make a hole in the centre of the top and place towards top of hot oven. Cook 15 min to brown pastry, reduce heat to 180°C, 350°F, Mark 4 and cook for a further 1¼–1½ hours, placing foil over if pastry gets too brown. Traditionally the pie would be served with two pigeons' feet placed in the hole just before serving, but a fresh sprig of parsley may appeal more.

4 helpings

SOMERSET CHICKEN
4 chicken portions
Seasoned flour
3 oz butter
1 level dessertsp dried thyme, rosemary, sage and tarragon
    mixed together
¼ pt dry cider
Salt and pepper
Watercress for garnish

Toss the chicken joints in seasoned flour. Melt the butter in a large frying pan, seal the chicken in the butter until golden, sprinkle the mixed herbs over the joints and cover the pan. Cook over low heat until chicken is tender. Place joints on a warmed serving dish. Pour the cider in the pan, mix with the pan juices, season with salt and pepper to taste, and when hot pour sauce over the chicken. Serve garnished with watercress.

4 helpings

CHARLTON CHICKEN
1 medium-sized onion, chopped
1 oz butter
4 chicken joints
1 tablesp chopped fennel
1 teasp chopped parsley
Salt and pepper
½ pt dry white wine
½ pt chicken stock
2 egg yolks beaten with 2 tablesp strained lemon juice *or*
    cornflour blended with cold water

Soften onion in melted butter, remove onion and brown chicken joints. Return onion to the pan and add all the other ingredients except the egg yolks, put lid on pan, bring to boil and simmer until chicken is cooked (about 45 min). Remove pan from heat and add egg yolk mixture, or thicken gravy with blended cornflour.

4 helpings

84

CELTIC DUCKLING

1 duckling, 4½–5½ lb (if frozen leave until thoroughly thawed)
Salt and pepper
2 tablesp cold water
2 oz butter
12 small onions
3 rashers bacon, de-rinded and chopped
1 sprig summer savory *or* rosemary
¼ pt giblet stock

Pre-heat oven to 180°C, 350°F, Mark 4. Prepare bird, rub salt into the skin, sprinkle a little salt and pepper inside the bird. Lay breast downwards on the rack in a roasting tin, add 2 tablesp water to the tin. Allow 25–30 min per lb cooking time. Turn bird over after 45 min. Melt butter in a pan, lightly fry onions until golden, add chopped bacon and fry, tossing or shaking pan for 3 min. 45 min before end of cooking time pour off most of fat in roasting tin, add the onions and bacon, put small pieces of savory or rosemary around, sprinkle in salt and pepper, pour in the stock and continue cooking.

Served garnished as you like.

6 helpings

Savoury
and Egg Dishes

SAVOURY CHEESE AND ONION FLAN
6 oz shortcrust pastry
½ oz butter
1 medium-sized onion, chopped
4 oz cheese, grated
2 eggs
½ teasp chopped fresh savory *or*
    a pinch of dried savory
Salt and pepper
¼ pt single cream

Pre-heat oven 200°C, 400°F, Mark 6. Line a 7-in flan ring, placed on a baking sheet, with pastry. Melt butter in a frying pan, fry chopped onion until softened but not browned, remove from pan, drain. Mix cheese, eggs, savory, salt, pepper and cream together in a bowl, using a whisk or fork. Cover base of flan with the onion, pour over the egg mixture and bake towards the top of oven for about 30 min, until filling is set and pastry cooked through. Serve hot.

6 helpings

POACHED EGGS WITH SORREL
1 lb very young sorrel leaves, any discoloured ones removed
Salt and pepper
2 tablesp double cream *or* small knob of butter
4 poached eggs

Wash sorrel and cook in the water clinging to the leaves (no other water) with lid on the pan for about 15 minutes. Drain, chop finely, add seasonings and butter or cream, cook gently, stirring, for 5 min. Place in a warm dish, top with poached eggs and serve piping hot.

4 helpings

ANCHOVIES AND SPAGHETTI
2 tablesp oil
1 oz butter
1 clove garlic, crushed
1 lb tomatoes, roughly chopped
Sprig of basil
1 small onion, chopped
4 anchovies, pounded
Salt and pepper
6–8 oz freshly-cooked spaghetti
Grated cheese

Mix butter and oil in a frying pan, add garlic, tomatoes, onion and basil, cover and cook gently, shaking occasionally, for 20 min, add pounded anchovies, and cook for a further 10 minutes; sieve, season to taste, re-heat and serve with the hot spaghetti. Hand grated cheese separately.

3 helpings

STUFFED HERBY EGGS
1 large slice wholemeal bread
4 eggs, hard-boiled
3 oz cream cheese
1 oz butter
A little cream, if necessary
Fresh marjoram, *or* dried, to taste
Fresh parsley sprigs

Cut bread into four small rounds. Cut eggs lengthwise, remove yolks. Place yolks, cream cheese and butter in a basin, beat until mixture is smooth, adding a little cream if required. Stir in marjoram to taste. Spoon or pipe most of the mixture into the egg cases, spread the remaining filling on the bread rounds. Stand one egg on each piece of bread; garnish the tops with small parsley sprigs.

4 helpings

CLASSIC OMELET AUX FINES HERBES
3 eggs
3 teasp cold water
Salt and pepper
½ oz butter
1 rounded tablesp chopped mixed parsley, chives, tarragon
  and chervil

Put pan over low heat to get hot. Break eggs into a basin, add water, salt, pepper and herbs. Beat lightly. Put butter in the pan, allow butter to sizzle but not turn brown, then pour in omelet mixture. Draw mixture from the sides to the middle of the pan with a fork, palette knife or wooden spatula, repeat until all the runny egg is lightly cooked. Fold over and serve.

There are many herb mixtures that can be added to a basic omelet, and for something different try chopped chervil and mint mixed together.

1 helping

EGGS WITH A DIFFERENCE
1 teasp chopped parsley
1 teasp chopped mint
4 oz lean cooked ham *or* cold boiled bacon, finely chopped
About 1 oz butter
6 eggs
Salt
Paprika pepper
Hot buttered toast

Pre-heat oven to 180°C, 350°F, Mark 4. Mix herbs with the ham or bacon. Generously butter six small, deep patty pans, dariole moulds or small cups. Sprinkle herb mixture thickly round bottom and sides, shaking out any that does not stick. Carefully break an egg into each container, sprinkle with salt, paprika pepper and top with a small dot of butter. Place containers in roasting tin or on a baking sheet and cook in centre of oven until eggs are set – about 8 min. Turn out carefully on to small pieces of buttered toast.

3–6 helpings

HEFTY OMELET

1 tablesp top-of-the-milk
1 tablesp chopped chives
1 oz full fat soft cheese
3 tablesp cold water
Salt and pepper
3 eggs, lightly beaten
About ½ oz butter
Small sprig parsley

Stir top-of-the-milk and chives into the cream cheese. Stir water and seasoning into the eggs. Melt butter in a 7-in omelet pan and when it is sizzling (do not let it brown), pour in egg mixture; cook omelet in usual way. Place cream cheese mixture across the centre, fold over one-third of the omelet away from the handle of pan, hold the handle, palm upwards, shake the omelet forward and turn out, making another fold, on to a warm plate. Garnish with a sprig of parsley and serve immediately.

1 large helping

SAVOURY RICE

6 oz brown, unpolished rice
1 dessertsp chopped mixed fresh herbs
2 large carrots, grated
1 Spanish onion, finely chopped
Chicken stock (can be made with stock cubes)
Strongly-flavoured grated cheese

Thoroughly wash the rice, place in saucepan, or double boiler, with the herbs, carrots and onion. Cover with boiling chicken stock. Put lid on pan and cook, adding a little more stock if necessary, until the rice is tender, by which time it should be soft and separate and the liquid absorbed (about 45—55 minutes). Serve with a stew or on its own, accompanied by a strongly-flavoured grated cheese.

N.B. If white, polished rice is used, cooking time 15—20 min.

3—4 helpings

Salads

SORREL SALAD
1 lb fresh, young sorrel leaves, washed and dried
6 pickled walnuts
Oil and lemon dressing

Remove stalks from sorrel, remove any wilted or tough leaves, and chop them finely. Chop four walnuts, mix with the leaves, toss in dressing, put in salad bowl and garnish with remaining walnuts cut in slices.

4 helpings

N.B.   To make **oil and lemon dressing**, use
1 part fresh lemon juice to 3 parts olive oil.
A simple recipe is:
1 tablesp lemon juice
3 tablesp olive oil
½ teasp salt
¼ teasp black pepper

Put lemon juice in a bowl, add salt and pepper, then the oil – shake or mix thoroughly.

For an oil and vinegar dressing, substitute malt, wine or cider vinegar for the lemon juice. To vary add 1 crushed garlic clove, a pinch of sugar and 1 teasp finely-chopped tarragon to the dressing.

TOMATO SALAD
4 firm tomatoes, skinned and sliced
Oil and vinegar dressing (see sorrel salad)
1 level dessertsp basil, freshly chopped, *or* chives

Cover sliced tomatoes with oil and vinegar dressing and leave to marinade in a cool place for at least 30 min. Lift slices from marinade into individual dishes and serve sprinkled with basil or chives.

2–4 helpings

90

RED CABBAGE SALAD
1 small *or* half a large red cabbage
1 small onion, chopped
2 sticks celery, chopped
Oil and vinegar dressing
1 rounded tablesp chopped parsley

Remove tough outer leaves and stalk of cabbage. Wash the cabbage, drain thoroughly and shred finely. Mix well with the onion and celery and toss in oil and vinegar dressing. Place in salad bowl and sprinkle the parsley over. This is an attractive winter salad to which you can add your own variations.

4 helpings

COS LETTUCE AND HERBS
1 very fresh cos lettuce
1 teasp each chopped tarragon, chervil and chives, *or* to taste
Oil and vinegar dressing

Wash lettuce, discarding any tough leaves and thick stalk. Dry leaves well and cut long ones into four or five pieces. Mix herbs together. Place a layer of lettuce in the base of a fairly shallow dish, sprinkle herbs over and some oil and vinegar dressing. Continue in this way until all the lettuce is in the bowl, reserving some of the herbs for the top layer. How much oil and vinegar dressing is used depends on personal taste.

6—8 helpings

SCARLET SALAD
½ lb sweet dark red cherries, stoned and halved
½ lb cold, cooked beetroot, diced
1 x 5-oz carton soured cream
Lemon balm leaves, chopped

Mix cherries and beetroot into the soured cream, chill and serve garnished with lemon balm.

4—6 helpings

MINTED PEA SALAD
1 round lettuce
12 oz cold, cooked peas

Dressing:
2 tablesp wine vinegar
½ teasp salt
Black pepper to taste
1 teasp caster sugar
6 tablesp olive oil
2 tablesp finely-chopped mint

Make the dressing first. Put the vinegar into a basin, add the salt, pepper and sugar, mix well, then add the oil. Mix thoroughly, or place in a beaker that has a lid and shake, finally add the mint and stir or shake again. Wash lettuce, dry carefully and arrange the young curled leaves on four serving plates. Toss the peas, which should be young, tender and not over-cooked, in the dressing, and pile them on to the lettuce leaves. (This is a delicious accompaniment to cold, roast lamb.)

4 helpings

Vegetables

DUTCH CABBAGE
About ¼ pt water
1 medium-sized white cabbage, shredded
3 rashers streaky bacon, cooked and chopped
½ teasp caraway seeds in muslin bag
Salt and pepper
Butter

Bring water to the boil, add cabbage, bacon and seeds mixed together, sprinkle seasoning over and put lid on pan. Cook until cabbage is beginning to soften (about 20 min). Drain, remove seeds, toss in the butter and serve.

6 helpings

RATATOUILLE

2 tablesp olive oil
1 oz butter
6 young courgettes, unpeeled, cut into small slices
1 lb aubergines, peeled and diced *or* thinly sliced
6 tomatoes, skinned and sliced
½ teasp chopped marjoram *or* basil
Salt and black pepper
1 clove garlic, crushed (optional)
5−6 coriander seeds, pounded

Heat oil and butter together gently, add vegetables, herbs and seasoning, garlic and coriander seeds, cover and cook over low heat until mixture is soft and just beginning to turn mushy. (If the oven is being used ratatouille can be cooked low down in a slow oven.)

4−6 helpings

TRADITIONAL BROAD BEANS AND SAVORY

1 oz butter
1 small onion, finely chopped
1 clove garlic, crushed
White stock *or* water to cover
    (about 1 pt)
2 lb young broad beans, podded
1 dessertsp chopped parsley
1−2 teasp chopped savory
Salt and pepper
Butter, cream *or* soured cream

Melt butter and gently fry onions and garlic in a thick saucepan until the onions have softened. Meanwhile bring 1 pt stock or water to the boil. Pour boiling liquid over onions, add beans, herbs and seasoning, cover and simmer until tender (about 20 min). Drain off surplus liquid – this can be used for soup – and toss beans in butter, cream or soured cream.

4−6 helpings

RED CABBAGE CASSEROLE
2 oz lard
1 medium-sized red cabbage, shredded, washed and drained
3 medium-sized red-skinned dessert apples, cored and diced
2 oz Demerara sugar
4 tablesp cider vinegar
¼ pt water
½ level teasp caraway seeds *or* to taste, tied in muslin bag
Salt and pepper

Melt lard in a large pan, add all the ingredients mixed together. Cover and cook over gentle heat, stirring from time to time, for 20–25 min, or longer if you prefer a softer texture. Remove seeds. Turn into heated serving dish.

8–10 helpings

IRISH POTATO CAKES
1 lb mashed potatoes
2 egg yolks
Salt
1 teasp chopped tansy
1 oz butter, melted
Plain flour
Fat for frying
Chopped parsley

Beat, sieve or blend the potatoes until they are very smooth, add the yolks, salt, tansy and melted butter, with sufficient flour to make a firm dough. Roll out on a lightly-floured board to ½-inch thickness, cut into small cakes 1½-in across, sprinkle flour over top and bottom and fry until lightly browned on one side. Turn and fry the other side. Serve piping hot, garnished with chopped parsley. Very good with pork.

4 helpings

POTATOES WITH DILL
1 lb small new potatoes, scraped
1 oz butter
1–2 teasp finely chopped dill

Boil and drain potatoes. As soon as drained return to pan, add butter and chopped dill and shake pan over very low heat until each potato is coated. Serve.

3–4 helpings

GARLIC POTATOES
8 medium-sized potatoes, peeled
3 oz butter
2–3 cloves garlic, crushed
Salt and pepper
Freshly-chopped parsley for garnish

Cut each potato into fairly thick slices, but take care not to cut right through to the base. Stand each potato on a square of kitchen foil. Melt butter, stir in garlic, salt and pepper. Pour melted butter over the potatoes, making sure it gets in between each slice. Make the foil into loose parcels, seal edges. Place in centre of oven at 220°C, 425°F, Mark 7, for 40–45 min, until the potatoes are cooked. Serve garnished with parsley.

4–8 helpings

DORSET POTATOES
1 lb mashed potatoes
½ bunch watercress, finely chopped
½ teasp freshly chopped savory, *or* a pinch if dried
½ oz butter
Salt and pepper

Beat all ingredients together and serve very hot.

4 helpings

CREAMED NETTLES
About 1 lb young nettle tops
1 oz butter
Pinch thyme
2 tablesp water
Salt and pepper
1 tablesp fresh breadcrumbs

Wash and shake dry nettle tops. Put butter, thyme, water, seasoning and nettles in saucepan, cover and cook over low heat until tender (about 25 min). Sprinkle breadcrumbs in base of warmed serving bowl, chop nettles but do not drain. Turn out over breadcrumbs and serve piping hot.

2—3 helpings

FRIED PARSLEY AS GARNISH
Fresh young sprigs of parsley as required, washed and patted dry
Deep fat

Choose parsley sprigs without thick stalks. When you have deep fried your main course, remove fat from heat and allow it to cool slightly (about 2—3 min), toss in the parsley, cook for about a minute, drain and serve. Fried parsley is crisp in texture and bright in colour. Very attractive on fried fish. Always stand back as you lower parsley in mesh basket into the fat, as it splutters and spits.

Puddings and Sweets

HAREM JELLY
1 pkt orange jelly
¾ pt water
4 eau-de-cologne mint leaves

Bring ½ pt water to the boil, pour over mint leaves, leave until cool, strain. Make up packet jelly using remaining water, add mint-flavoured water, pour into wetted mould, leave to set.

4—5 helpings

Cooking without herbs is almost unthinkable now that herbs are so readily available

The almost devilish look of herb wines does not belie their potency

COUNTRY FRUIT SALAD

4 oz each red cherries, raspberries, strawberries, pears, dessert apples
½ lb sugar
1 pt water
1 tablesp lemon juice
6 slightly-crushed pineapple-mint leaves

Stone the cherries. Dissolve sugar in the water, bring to boil, simmer for 2–3 min. Add peeled, cored and sliced apples and pears, poach until almost tender, then add the cherries. Cook for 1–2 min, finally add raspberries and strawberries and cook for 1 min more. Transfer to a serving bowl, with the lemon juice and pineapple-mint leaves. Leave, covered, to get quite cold. Remove mint leaves and serve salad with whipped cream or thick cold custard.

5–6 helpings

GRANDMOTHER'S RICE PUDDING

1 pt milk
1 bay leaf
1½ oz pudding rice
1½ oz sugar
½ oz butter

Warm milk and bay leaf in a pan, but do not boil; leave to get cool. Remove bay leaf. Wash rice in cold water. Grease an ovenproof dish. Put rice, sugar, milk and butter into dish, stir well and cook, low in the oven at 150°C, 300°F, Mark 2, for 2 or 3 hr. After about 35 min stir in the skin, as this helps to give a creamier-tasting pudding.

Rice pudding can also be cooked on top of the stove, if preferred.

4–6 helpings

VERBENA CUSTARD
3–4 lemon verbena leaves
2 pt milk
Peel of ½ lemon, grated
4 oz caster sugar
6 eggs, lightly beaten

Put lemon verbena leaves, peel and milk into a saucepan and leave in a warm place for flavours to infuse (about 30 min). Strain and cool. Stir in sugar and eggs. Strain into a jug or double saucepan. Place jug in a deep pan of boiling water, put on low heat and stir until custard thickens. (More verbena leaves, or bay leaves, can be used if preferred.)

N.B. This custard should be served as soon as it is ready.

6 helpings

WESTMORLAND MINTY PASTRY
Rich short pastry

8 oz flour sifted with ½ teasp salt
5 oz margarine
½ oz sugar
Water to mix

For filling

2 oz butter
2 oz soft brown sugar
4 oz currants
2 good tablesp chopped mint
Water
Caster sugar

Pre-heat oven to 200°C, 400°F, Mark 6. Rub fat into flour until the breadcrumb stage, mix in sugar, then sufficient water to make a firm dough. Turn out on to floured board. Divide pastry into two and roll each piece into a square. Leave in a cool place while you prepare the filling.

Cream butter and sugar, stir in currants and mint, mix thoroughly. Place one square of pastry on a baking sheet.

Brush round edges with water. Spread currant filling evenly in the middle. Top with second pastry square. Seal edges and crimp decoratively. Cut 3 or 4 slits in top. Brush with water and sprinkle caster sugar over. Bake just above centre of oven for 20–25 min.

6 helpings

APPLE TANSY
3 large cooking apples, peeled, cored and sliced
3–4 tablesp water
1 small sprig tansy, chopped
¼ pt double cream, lightly whipped
2 egg yolks, lightly beaten
Sugar *or* honey to taste

Cook apples with water and tansy over gentle heat until soft and dry (take care they do not brown). Cool slightly. Stir in cream, egg yolks and sugar to taste, return to heat and cook slowly, stirring, until thick. Turn out and serve either hot or cold.

4 helpings

RASPBERRY CRUMBLE
Sugar to taste
1 lb hulled raspberries

For topping

6 oz self-raising flour
½–1 teasp crushed coriander seeds
3 oz butter *or* margarine
2 oz sugar

Pre-heat oven 200°C, 400°F, Mark 6. Mix sugar into raspberries and place in an ovenproof dish. Sieve flour and powdered seeds and rub in fat until the breadcrumb stage, mix in sugar. Spread crumble mixture over fruit and bake in oven for 20–25 min, until topping is golden. Serve hot or cold with whipped cream.

4 helpings

APPLE SWEET
4 medium-sized cooking apples
Water
2 sprigs eau-de-cologne mint
Brown sugar

Core but do not peel the apples and put them with approximately 1-in depth water, mint and 1 tablesp sugar in a saucepan. Cover and simmer until tender. Do not over-cook, or allow to become mushy. Add more water is necessary. Drain and serve with brown sugar piled into core cavities and sprinkled over.

4 helpings

TRAFFIC LIGHT PUDDING
A little oil
2 oz glacé cherries
3 oz semolina
1½ pts milk
4 oz sugar
¼ oz gelatine
1 x 8-oz can pineapple chunks
4 tablesp syrup from canned fruit
1 rounded dessertsp chopped angelica
Grated rind of 1 orange
Angelica for garnish
1 egg white

Lightly oil a 2-pint mould or bowl, using a tasteless oil. Arrange some of the cherries, cut into halves, at the base. Put semolina, milk and sugar into a saucepan and stir over a low heat until mixture comes to the boil. Allow it to simmer, still stirring, for 8−10 min. Remove from heat, leave it to cool for about 5 min. In the meantime dissolve gelatine in 4 tablesp fruit syrup, add it to the semolina. Reserving five cherries, chop the rest, mix with the chopped angelica and grated orange rind, stir into semolina. Whisk the egg white stiffly and fold in. Pour mixture into prepared mould, leave to set. Turn out and decorate with remaining cherries and angelica, and place the pineapple chunks around.

6−8 helpings

Cakes, Biscuits and Breads

HOT HERBY LOAF

1 heaped tablesp chopped mixed herbs *or*
  1 level tablesp chopped parsley and
  fennel mixed
Salt and pepper
3 oz unsalted butter, creamed
1 small loaf bread

Mix herbs and seasoning into butter. Cut loaf into ½-in slices
lengthwise, but not through to the final crust. Spread each
side of the slices with butter. Wrap in foil and 'cook' in a hot
oven for about 10 minutes. Serve warm.

GARLIC BREAD
1 French loaf
2–3 cloves garlic, crushed
Creamed butter as required

Cut loaf crosswise, taking care not to cut through final crust. Then treat like herby loaf.

DAFFY'S SODA BREAD
1 lb plain flour
1 level teasp salt
1 level teasp bicarbonate of soda
1 rounded teasp of cream of tartar
1 oz butter
1 scant dessertsp dill seeds
½ pt milk

Pre-heat oven to 220°C, 425°F, Mark 7. Sift flour, salt, bicarbonate of soda and cream of tartar into a basin. Rub in fat. Stir in dill seeds. Mix in the milk to make a soft dough, and knead mixture lightly until it is smooth. Form into a round on a floured baking tray. Cut 4 diagonal lines across top, prick all over with a fork and cook towards top of hot oven for 30–35 min.

PLAIN SEED CAKE
8 oz self-raising flour
4 oz margarine
¼ teasp salt
4 oz caster sugar
1 oz caraway seeds
2 eggs
Milk to mix

Pre-heat oven to 180°C, 350°F, Mark 4. Line a greased 7-in cake tin with greased greaseproof paper. Sieve flour and salt, rub in margarine. Stir in sugar and seeds. Beat eggs with a little milk. Make a well in the centre of cake mix, pour in eggs. Slowly work dry ingredients into the eggs, adding more milk until a soft dropping consistency is obtained. Put into cake tin, level top and bake for about 1–1¼ hours, until cooked through.

PEASANT BREAD

About 1½ pt water
1 oz dried yeast
2 lb wholemeal flour
1 lb plain white flour
1 oz salt
2 oz lard
1 level tablesp fennel seeds
1 oz sugar

Warm ¼ pt of the water to blood heat. Sprinkle in the yeast, whisk lightly, leave in warm place for 10–15 min, until yeast has dissolved and top is bubbly. Mix the flours and salt together. Rub in the fat. Stir in seeds and sugar. Make a well in the middle, pour in yeast mixture and most of the water. Stir until a soft dough is formed, adding a little more water if required. Knead until smooth, leave to rise until doubled in size. Meanwhile, grease 3 1-lb loaf tins, then dust them with flour. Turn dough on to lightly-floured board. Knead and put into tins. Leave to prove until tins are full. Bake near top of oven at 230°C, 450°F, Mark 8 for 15 min, reduce heat to 200°C, 400°F, Mark 6 and cook for a further 40–50 min, or until loaves sound 'hollow'.

CARAWAY BISCUITS

8 oz flour
Pinch of salt
½ teasp cinnamon
3 oz butter
3 oz caster sugar
1 level teasp caraway seeds
1 large egg yolk
Egg and caster sugar to sprinkle over

Pre-heat oven to 190°C, 375°F, Mark 5. Sift flour, salt and cinnamon into a bowl, rub in the fat, stir in sugar and seeds. Add beaten egg yolk and knead well. Roll out into ¼-in thick rounds, brush with a little beaten egg, sprinkle sugar over and bake over centre of oven for 10–15 min.

Yield approximately 24 biscuits

VICARAGE BISCUITS
4 oz margarine
4 oz caster sugar
1 egg
8 oz plain flour
1 level teasp caraway seeds

Pre-heat oven to 180°C, 350°F, Mark 4. Cream margarine and sugar until light and fluffy, beat in egg a little at a time, then add flour and caraway seeds. Mix to a firm dough, roll out to ¼-in thickness on a lightly-floured board. Cut out into star shapes with a cutter about 2½-in diameter and bake above centre of oven for 15 min, when the biscuits should be firm, and light brown in colour.

Yield approximately 20 biscuits

GINGERBREAD
1 teasp crushed coriander seeds
4 tablesp water
1 lb plain flour
½ teasp salt
1 level tablesp ground ginger
1 level tablesp baking powder
¾ level teasp bicarbonate of soda
8 oz soft brown sugar
4 oz black treacle
8 oz golden syrup
½ pt milk, less 4 tablesp
1 egg, beaten

Warm the water, pour over seeds, leave to infuse and cool for about 30 min. Pre-heat oven to 170°C, 325°F, Mark 3. Line an 8-in square tin with greased greaseproof paper. Sift flour with salt, ginger, baking powder and bicarbonate of soda. Warm together the sugar, treacle and syrup until melted and runny but do not allow to boil. Cool a little if necessary and pour in milk, coriander water and egg. Make a well in flour mixture, pour in syrup liquid and, using a wooden spoon, mix all ingredients thoroughly together. Pour into tin. Bake in centre of oven for about 1½ hours, or until firm.

SAVOURY BISCUITS
3 oz plain flour
2 oz fine oatmeal
½ teasp dry mixed herbs *or* 1 teasp chopped fresh herbs
Salt and pepper
2 oz margarine *or* butter
2 oz grated cheddar cheese
1 egg, lightly beaten

Pre-heat oven to 190°C, 375°F, Mark 5. Mix flour, oats, seasoning and herbs in a basin, rub in fat, stir in cheese. Add sufficient egg to make a firm dough. Roll out thinly on a floured board, use a 3-in cutter to make the biscuits. Place on lightly-greased baking sheet. Brush over with remaining egg. Cook in centre of oven for about 15 min. Cool on wire tray.

Yield 15–18 biscuits

RICH SEED CAKE
8 oz self-raising flour
Pinch of salt
½ teasp cinnamon
¼ teasp nutmeg
1 level dessertsp caraway seeds
6 oz unsalted butter
6 oz caster sugar
3 eggs, beaten
Milk to mix

Pre-heat oven to 180°C, 350°F, Mark 4. Prepare cake tin as for Plain Seed Cake. Sieve flour, salt, cinnamon and nutmeg. Stir in the seeds. Cream butter and sugar until light and fluffy, beat in the eggs a little at a time, then fold in the flour. Add sufficient milk to make a soft dropping consistency. Bake just below centre of oven for 1–1¼ hours, until cooked through.

Sauces and Dressings

CUCUMBER SAUCE FOR FISH
½ oz unsalted butter
1 large cucumber, peeled and cut into ¾-in chunks
Salt and pepper
Chopped dill *or* fennel

Melt butter, add cucumber, cover pan and simmer, shaking pan frequently, until cucumber is just tender (about 7–10 min). Season to taste and serve garnished with chopped dill or fennel.

DILLY APPLE SAUCE
1 lb cooking apples, peeled, cored and sliced
2 tablesp water
½–1 oz sugar
A small knob of unsalted butter
1 dessertsp freshly-chopped dill

Cook apples with water over gentle heat until soft and dry, add sugar and butter, beat or sieve until smooth and stir in the dill. Serve hot or cold. This sauce makes an easy filling for an omelet.

ELIZABETHAN SAUCE FOR PORK
1½ lb cooking apples, peeled, cored and sliced
½ lb quince, peeled, cored and sliced
2–3 tablesp water
Juice of 1 lemon
1–2 oz sugar
2 oz butter
1 rounded tablesp freshly-chopped mint

Put apples, quince, water, lemon juice and sugar in a pan, simmer until soft and dry, taking care the mixture does not burn. Stir in butter, heat or sieve until smooth, then add the mint. Re-heat very gently, if necessary. (Very good with bacon, sausages and goose as well as pork.)

BÉCHAMEL SAUCE
1 pt milk
½ small carrot
1 shallot *or* small onion
1 small *or* ½ large bay leaf
Bouquet garni
6 peppercorns
2 oz butter
1½ oz flour
6 tablesp single cream
Salt and pepper

Put milk, carrot, shallot, herbs and peppercorns into a saucepan, bring to the boil, remove from heat, cover and leave for 30 min for flavours to blend. Strain. Melt butter in a pan, stir in flour, cook for two minutes, slowly add strained milk, stirring all the time. Bring to the boil, cook for two minutes, remove from heat. Add cream and season to taste.

FENNEL SAUCE FOR FISH
1 rounded tablesp finely-chopped fennel
Salt and pepper
1 x 5-oz carton soured cream
Sugar to taste

Mix all ingredients together, whisking lightly with a fork. If time permits, cover and leave for a little while for flavours to blend.

HOT HORSERADISH SAUCE
½ oz butter
½ oz plain flour
½ pt milk
Salt and white pepper
4 level tablesp grated horseradish
1 dessertsp white wine vinegar
1 level dessertsp caster sugar

Melt butter, cook flour in saucepan for 2 min. Slowly add the milk, stirring all the time, bring to boil, cook, stirring for 2 min. Remove from heat. Add the other ingredients. Left-over sauce can be used cold.

QUICK HORSERADISH SAUCE
¼ pt cream
3 level tablesp grated horseradish
1 dessertsp white wine vinegar
Salt and pepper

Lightly whip the cream, stir in horseradish and vinegar, adding salt and pepper to taste. Leave in a cool place until ready. Use within 24 hours.

MINTED GOOSEBERRY JELLY
2 lb small, hard green cooking gooseberries
Cold water
Sugar
6–8 sprigs of mint, tied in a bundle

Put berries in a thick pan, cover with water, cook until soft. Strain through a jelly bag; do not squeeze to hurry process. Measure liquid, allow 1 lb sugar per pt of liquid. Put sugar and liquid in pan, add mint, heat, stirring, until sugar has dissolved, then boil rapidly until setting point is reached. Remove mint and pour jelly into warmed and sterilized small jars. Seal.

TARTARE SAUCE
½ pt mayonnaise
1 teasp each chopped parsley, capers, tarragon, chervil, gherkins
¼ teasp sugar

Put mayonnaise into a bowl, stir in all the other ingredients, cover and allow to steep for at least 30 min before serving.

ALMOST INSTANT DRESSING
1 x 5-oz carton natural yogurt
Salt and pepper
1 rounded tablesp any mixed chopped herbs

Mix altogether and use as a salad dressing (good for slimmers).

MINT SAUCE
Mint sprigs, washed and dried
Sugar
Boiling water
White *or* malt vinegar

Place mint leaves on a chopping board with one or two fine young pieces of stem. Sprinkle 2 teasp sugar over and chop finely, (the sugar helps to absorb oils from the mint). To every rounded tablespoon chopped mint add, in a bowl, one level teasp sugar and pour over 1 tablesp boiling water. Stir to dissolve sugar, then pour in vinegar to taste. Leave to infuse for at least an hour before serving.

PARSLEY SAUCE
1 dessertsp chopped parsley
½ oz butter
½ oz plain flour
½ pt milk less 1 tablesp
1 tablesp single cream
Salt and pepper

Wash, chop and carefully dry the parsley (if it is wet it will discolour the sauce). Melt butter, cook flour in saucepan for 2 minutes. Slowly stir in milk, bring to boil, stirring, cook 2 minutes. Season to taste. Remove from heat, stir in cream and parsley.

HORSERADISH AND BEETROOT RELISH
½ lb cooked, cold beetroot, peeled and finely chopped *or* grated
4 oz grated horseradish
1 rounded tablesp caster sugar
¼ teasp salt
¼ pt white vinegar

Mix ingredients thoroughly. Put in jar. Cover. Can be used after 1 hour and will keep for up to 3 weeks if stored in a cool place.

Stuffings

APPLE, SAGE AND ONION STUFFING
2 medium-sized cooking apples, peeled, cored and sliced
2 medium-sized onions, sliced
3 thyme leaves
4 sage leaves
Cold water
Approximately 2 tablesp mashed potato
Salt and black pepper

Place apples and onions in a saucepan with herb leaves. Barely cover with water and cook over low heat until tender. Drain off surplus liquid, sieve or blend, and season with salt and pepper. Stir in sufficient mashed potato to make mixture dry and smooth (use for stuffing duck or goose).

CHESTNUT STUFFING
1 lb chestnuts
2 oz unsalted butter
2 oz fresh white breadcrumbs
½ lb pork sausagemeat
½ teasp dried thyme *or*
    1 teasp fresh thyme leaves *or*
    1 teasp fresh marjoram
½ teasp dried marjoram
½ teasp chopped parsley
Milk
Salt and pepper

Score the chestnuts with a sharp kitchen knife, place them in a hot oven for a few minutes to loosen the skins. Remove all the skins and place chestnuts in a saucepan. Just cover with milk. Lay a piece of buttered greaseproof paper over and put the lid on the pan. Bring milk to boil, then simmer gently until nuts are tender. Drain off remaining milk. Sieve nuts and mix in the butter. Leave to get cold. Mix breadcrumbs, sausagemeat, herbs and seasoning into the chestnut purée (use for stuffing turkey, etc).

PARSLEY AND THYME STUFFING
4 oz fresh white breadcrumbs
1 oz shredded suet *or* butter, grated
1 level tablesp chopped parsley
1 level dessertsp chopped thyme
Finely-grated rind of ½ lemon
Salt and pepper
1 egg, beaten
Milk to bind

Mix together all the ingredients, using sufficient milk to bind.

SAGE AND ONION STUFFING
4 onions, sliced
7 fresh sage leaves *or* 1 level dessertsp powdered sage
1 oz butter
Pepper and salt
4 oz soft breadcrumbs
Egg to bind

Simmer the onion in a little water until tender, drain and
chop. Add the sage, butter, seasoning, breadcrumbs and leave
to cool. Mix in sufficient beaten egg to bind.

STUFFING FOR VEAL
3 oz lean ham, minced *or* finely chopped
2 teasp chopped parsley
1 teasp chopped lemon thyme *or* lemon verbena (pinch of
    finely powdered if dried)
A pinch of marjoram
4 oz shredded suet
Salt and pepper
6 oz soft white breadcrumbs
2 eggs, lightly beaten

Mix first seven ingredients. Use sufficient egg to bind.

Herb Teas

There can be a bit of confusion about herb teas. Basically, they are like any other tea, only made with a herb of your choice. Sometimes they are known as Tisanes. They are also referred to as infusions. The latter more often implies that the tea is being regarded not just as a refreshing drink but is used for medicinal purposes or as an aid to beauty (see Chapter 9).

Drink herb tea as you would Indian or China tea, with or without milk, with or without lemon, with or without sweetening. Starting the day with herb tea or having one as a relaxing night-cap can be very soothing.

Always use a china or glass container when making a herb tea. Keep it covered while the tea is 'brewing'. Trial and error will show which herbs you prefer and how much herb in the pot suits your taste. To begin with use three teasp freshly-chopped (or 1 teasp dried herb) for each pt of boiling water. Infuse 5–10 min. Or 1 level tablesp seeds, crushed or pounded, for each pt boiling water.

These recipes are for some of the best known teas, with suggested quantities to adapt to your taste.

112

CHAMOMILE TEA
10–12 chamomile flowers, less if dried
1 pt boiling water
Demerara sugar to taste

Cover flowers with boiling water, infuse 5 min, sweeten. Strain.

1–2 helpings

MINT TEA
(Suitable for common or pineapple mint)
3 teasp freshly-chopped mint, *or* 1 teasp dried mint
½ pt boiling water
Sugar to taste

Pour boiling water over the chopped mint, leave to infuse for 3–5 min. Strain and sweeten.

1 helping

SAGE TEA
Make as mint tea.

EAU-DE-COLOGNE TEA
2 teasp freshly-chopped eau-de-cologne mint
1 teasp freshly-chopped lemon verbena, quarter quantities if
   dried
½ pt boiling water
Sugar to sweeten

Pour boiling water over the mixed chopped herbs. Infuse 4–5 min, strain, sweeten.

ICED MINT TEA
Tea – China tea best
Crushed mint leaves
Ice cubes
Thinly-cut lemon slices

Make tea in your usual way, sweeten to taste, leave to get cold. Put 3 or 4 crushed mint leaves in the bottom of a glass, top with ice cubes, strain tea over, garnish with lemon slices.

BERGAMOT TEA
3 teasp China or Indian tea
3 leaves bergamot, slightly crushed
1½ pt boiling water

Make tea in the usual way, adding bergamot leaves, infuse 5–10 min.

OSWEGO TEA
4 teasp freshly-chopped bergamot
1 pt boiling water
Sugar *or* honey to taste

Pour water over chopped leaves, infuse for 5–10 min, strain, sweeten and serve.

NETTLE TEA
4 teasp freshly-chopped young nettle leaves
1 teacup boiling water
Sugar to sweeten

Pour boiling water over the nettles, infuse 5 min, strain, sweeten.

Alcoholic Drinks

CLARET CUP
1 bottle claret
1 wineglass brandy
1 large bottle soda-water
1 lemon, cut into 4
2–3-in cucumber, sliced
3 sprigs borage
4 oz sugar
10 ice cubes

Put lemon and cucumber into a large jug with the sugar, soda-water, brandy and claret. Stir with a long spoon until sugar has dissolved, then add the borage. Cover and leave in the refrigerator for 1 hr. Strain. Add ice cubes and serve immediately. (If liked the Cup can be poured into a bowl and garnished with borage leaves and flowers.)

8–10 helpings

114

BORAGE CUP
1 pt cider
About ½ pt soda-water
Peel of ¼ cucumber
Thinly-pared skin of ½ lemon
1 sprig borage
2 liqueur glasses maraschino
1 liqueur glass brandy
Sugar to taste
Ice
Borage for decoration

Slightly crush the borage and mix all the ingredients in a jug, stirring until sugar has dissolved. Leave to blend for about an hour. Strain. Serve with ice and garnish with sprigs of borage

4—5 helpings

PORT WINE NEGUS
½ pt port
½ pt boiling water
About ⅓ whole nutmeg, 3 cloves, ¼ teasp caraway seeds,
    tied in a muslin bag
Sugar to taste

Put muslin bag with port in a saucepan, bring to boil, simmer 1—2 min, remove bag and pour boiling water into port, sweeten to taste and serve.

3 helpings

WHISKY JULEP
6 sprigs of mint
4 sugar lumps
4 tablesp whisky
More whisky to taste
Crushed ice

Put a sprig of mint, sugar lumps and tablesp whisky into each glass, and crush with a spoon. Cover glasses, and chill briefly. Then fill with crushed ice, pour in whisky to taste, stir, using a long-handled spoon to frost the glasses (don't touch outside of glass with your hands), then garnish with mint leaves and serve.

4 helpings

Non-Alcoholic Drinks

NETTLE COOLER
2 lb young nettles
4 pt water
Sugar
Soda-water

Bring nettles and water to boil in a covered pan. Reduce heat and cook gently for an hour. Strain, and measure liquid. Allow 1 lb sugar per pt, bring slowly to boil, cover and leave gently bubbling, for 30 min. Cool. Serve diluted with soda-water to taste. The syrup can be bottled and kept in a cool place, but is better made frequently.

NON-ALCOHOLIC APÉRITIF
Crushed mint sprigs
Bottled lime juice
Ice
Soda-water

Crush one or two mint sprigs in bottom of a glass, pour over about ½-in depth lime juice, add ice and fill glass with soda-water.

1 helping

116

PINEAPPLE FRUIT CAP
¼ pt pineapple juice
½ pt fresh orange juice
½ pt water
Grated rind and juice of 1 lemon
2 oz caster sugar *or* to taste
6 crushed pineapple mint leaves
2 pt ginger ale
Pineapple mint sprigs

Mix together first six ingredients, cover and leave in cool place for at least an hour for flavours to blend. Strain, add ginger ale, stir well, pour into glasses and serve decorated with pineapple mint sprigs.

7–10 helpings

CITRUS CUP
½ pt grapefruit juice
1 pt orange juice
¼ pt lemon juice
1 pt water
Sugar to taste
6–8 mint leaves, slightly crushed (pineapple mint leaves best)
Mint leaves or borage flowers for decoration

Mix together fruit juices and sugar, stir until sugar has dissolved, add remaining ingredients, chill. Decorate with mint leaves or borage flowers.

6–8 helpings

CHILDREN'S MINT JULEP
1 pt milk
2 oz bar milk chocolate
¼ teasp peppermint essence
1 tablesp whipped cream
Mint leaves

Warm the milk, dissolve the chocolate bar in it, add peppermint essence and allow to get cold. Pour into 2 or 3 glasses, top with whipped cream and decorate with mint leaves.

2–3 helpings

6
Herbs for Beauty and Health

Throughout the ages and all over the world women have tried to be as beautiful as possible. Herbs have been used to improve and even colour hair, whiten teeth, strengthen gums, brighten and soothe eyes, cleanse the skin, remove freckles and spots, get rid of wrinkles and relieve aching limbs, as well as to alleviate headaches, menstrual pains and minor ailments. Now there is a revival of interest in these time-tested methods which are easy to prepare and light on the purse.

Basically, what are needed most of the time are infusions (that is a standard herb tea, left to brew and then strained) or a herb oil.

To make a **herb oil** you need 2-oz. of finely-crushed herbs of choice (you can pound them or put them through a blender), 8 fl oz corn or olive oil, 1 tablsp wine vinegar. Place herbs in a bottle or glass jar, pour oil and vinegar over and leave in the sun or a warm room for two weeks, shaking the container hard once a day. After two weeks, strain through muslin, squeeze any oil out of the herbs and discard them; using fresh herbs, use the same oil again and repeat the process as many times as is needed to get the oil to the strength when it smells strongly of the herbs. A good test is to rub a little on the back of your hand. Lavender, fennel, rosemary, tarragon are very good herbs to use. Try to gather the herbs (leaf part only, unless you use seeds for a special mixture) in the summer. For decoration add a sprig of the dried herb to the final jar. Make a selection of oils, some for beauty, some to add to salad dressings and so on.

Hair is said to be a woman's crowning glory. Make it so for you. Rosemary, chamomile and sage are recommended for hair itself; parsley and nettles for the scalp.

If you are a brunette, pour a rosemary infusion over your hair; you can use fresh or dried leaves, for the final rinse. This will add lustre and a delicate perfume. Blondes should use a chamomile infusion, and for black hair a sage one is best. Rosemary oil is good for dry hair. If the hair is particularly dry, as for instance when you have been sunbathing overlong with your head uncovered, massage oil into the hair the night before shampooing. Cover your head, though, to save the pillow. For normally dry hair, rub oil into head 15 minutes before shampooing.

Another recommended oil for dry hair is made with nettle leaves.

A strong infusion of nettles massaged into the scalp is said to alleviate baldness and a standard nettle infusion, strained and rubbed into the scalp, is an old remedy for dandruff; so is a parsley infusion, which should be massaged hard into the scalp twice a week.

A clear skin is a boon. A daily drink of parsley tea is an old way of ensuring a healthy skin. A good cold cream helps too. Gently warm up in a pan an unscented cold cream, add a little herb oil of your choice, re-pot, leave to get cold; apply nightly.

To get rid of unsightly spots apply an infusion of sorrel or tansy on cotton wool. To remove freckles, mix one rounded tablespoon grated horseradish with one teacup milk, bring to boiling point, strain and cool. Apply to face with cotton wool, leave to dry, and rinse off with tepid water after ten minutes. Repeat every other day as long as is required, making fresh lotion as necessary.

A face pack is not a modern invention; mixed herb leaves, boiled in a little water, mashed, cooled and applied to the face have been used for centuries. Another mask is made with white of egg mixed with a little lemon juice and finely-chopped fennel leaves. Smooth over face, avoiding eyes and mouth, let dry, leave on 15 minutes, rinse off with tepid water.

The water in which you rinse your face has also been considered important by women over the years. Recommended rinses are strained rosemary or lemon balm infusions, cold or warmed up just before using, and left to dry on the face.

Tired or dull eyes mar beauty. An infusion of lemon verbena, carefully strained and cooled and applied in an eye bath, works wonders.

A stye on the eye is painful as well as ugly. An old cure is to apply an infusion of tansy to the sore morning and night. For a black eye (should such ill fortune come your way), or for a bruise, press on crushed hyssop leaves.

A relaxing bath can sooth away aches and pains. Add a little of your favourite herb oil and try out different ones, such as bergamot, to maintain a smooth skin.

Infusions can be added to bath water or fresh, or dried herbs, can be tied in a bag and held under the hot tap as the water runs in. A bag of marjoram is said to relieve stiffness and rheumatic pains. Fennel infusion or oil is an ancient slimming method. Sprigs of rosemary or lavender, or chamomile (flowers too), floating in the bath, are believed to be calming after a busy day, and mint in the bath is held to be invigorating. An infusion should be plentiful and strong: make it with about four oz leaves and four pt water.

Depending a great deal on how badly your feet ache and if you are alone or not, here is a remedy for badly aching feet. Rub the soles and heels with garlic cloves, sit with your feet up for a while and then rinse them in cool water.

Beautiful teeth are an asset; rubbing sage leaves over teeth and your gums is the herbal way of keeping teeth white, gums strong and healthy.

Just as herbs have long been valued for home-made beauty preparations, so they have been for medicinal purposes. But don't try to prescribe for yourself or for friends. In case of any possible or definite serious complaint, seek expert advice.

Infusions (teas) are usually taken for minor troubles.

Here are just a few of the well-known herbal remedies. When not taken as a 'tea', take in wineglassfuls, three times a day, either warmed up or cold.

120

ANGELICA:	Heartburn: 1-oz dried or fresh leaves and young stems, with one pint boiling water. Take about four tablespoons at a time. A longer drink is a pick-me-up.
BASIL:	Travel sickness, nausea: ½–1-oz dried leaves to 1 pt, boiling water. Take a sherry glass full before travelling.
BAY:	Sleeplessness: Put 1 or 2 bay leaves under your pillow.
BORAGE:	Beneficial to kidneys: Infusion as basil.
SALAD BURNET:	Cools blood, helps clear skin: Infusion as basil, or eat raw leaves.
CHAMOMILE:	Sleeplessness, see teas: Drink last thing at night. A cup of warm chamomile tea, sweetened with honey, relieves tiredness, and is a mild tranquiliser.
CHERVIL:	Tonic, good for memory: ½-oz dried or fresh leaves with 1 pint boiling water.
CORIANDER:	Indigestion: Chew a few seeds immediately before eating if prone to indigestion. Make an infusion with 3 teasp dried leaves or 1 teasp seeds per pt boiling water for indigestion.
DILL:	Flatulence: 2 teasp pounded seeds per ½ pt boiling water.
FENNEL:	Nerves, cough, tonic: Slightly bruise seeds then infuse as dill for coughs. Use 1-oz fresh leaves per pt boiling water as calming tonic.
GARLIC:	Believed good for pretty nearly everything: Strongly antiseptic rubbed raw on wounds; for chest complaints and colds chewed raw.
HYSSOP:	Catarrh: Standard infusion using 1-oz fresh young tops. Calming the nerves: Infusion with 1 teasp dried flowers, 1 pt boiling water, sweetened with honey.
LEMON BALM:	Soothing nerves: Eat raw, or as infusion (see balm tea).

LOVAGE:	Relieves menstrual strain: 3 teasp fresh leaves, or 2 dried per pint boiling water.
MARJORAM:	For nerves: Infusion as basil.
MINT:	Hiccoughs, indigestion: Chew mint leaves to cure hiccoughs: mint tea (see teas) for indigestion.
NETTLES:	Purify the blood: (See nettle tea).
PARSLEY:	Anaemia: Eat as much raw as possible. For skin: 3 teasp fresh or 1 dried, per pint boiling water.
ROSEMARY:	Menstrual pains, tenseness: Make infusion with 1-oz fresh young tops and leaves, or ½-oz dried, per pint of boiling water. Teacup daily.
SAGE:	Headaches, catarrh: Sage tea (see teas) for headaches. With honey for catarrh.
SORREL:	Swelling from fall: Crush sorrel leaves in hand and apply to spot, or crush and dab on juice.
TANSY:	Loss of appetite: Menopause flushes: 2 teasp fresh or 1 dried leaf per pint boiling water. Teacup daily.
THYME:	Bad breath, headaches: As basil.

Appendix:
Table of Weights and Measures

Liquid measures

60 drops	1 teasp
3 teaspoons	1 tablesp
4 tablespoons	½ gill
1 gill	¼ pt
4 gills	1 pt
2 pt	1 qt
4 qt	1 gal

Homely solid measures

All the spoons referred to in this book are British Standard teaspoons and tablespoons, which hold the amounts of liquid given above. They are measured with the contents levelled off, i.e. all the spoonfuls are level spoonfuls.

The cup is a British Standard measuring cup which holds 10 fluid oz or an Imperial ½ pint.

Homely solid measures

Flour, sifted	3 tablesp	1 oz
Castor or granulated sugar	2 tablesp	1¼ oz
Icing sugar, sifted	3 tablesp	1 oz
Butter or margarine	2 tablesp	1¼ oz
Cornflour	2 tablesp	1 oz
Granulated or powdered gelatine	4 teasp	½ oz

123

Homely solid measures / cont.

Golden syrup or treacle	1 tablesp	1 oz
Flour, sifted	1 cup	5 oz
Castor or granulated sugar	1 cup	9 oz
Icing sugar, sifted	1 cup	5 oz
Butter or margarine	1 cup	9 oz
Cornflour	1 cup	8 oz
Golden syrup or treacle	1 cup	1 lb

Metric measures

Precise metric equivalents are not very useful. The weights are almost impossible to measure accurately, and are not used in ordinary cooking. Schools use a 25-gram unit for 1 oz and for re-tested recipes. This means that they can use existing equipment. For instance, a 6-inch sandwich tin can be used for a 15-cm one, and a 7-inch tin for an 18-cm one. Yorkshire pudding using 100 grams plain flour fits into a 2 x 14 cm (8 in x 5½ in) baking tin.

Oven temperatures

	Electric	Celsius	Gas
Very cool	225°F	110°C	¼
Very cool	250°F	130°C	½
Very cool	275°F	140°C	1
Cool	300°F	150°C	2
Warm	325°F	170°C	3
Moderate	350°F	180°C	4
Fairly hot	375°F	190°C	5
Fairly hot	400°F	200°C	6
Hot	425°F	220°C	7
Very hot	450°F	230°C	8
Very hot	475°F	240°C	9

Deep fat frying table

Food	Bread Browns in	Fat Temp	Oil Temp
Raw starchy foods – doughnuts, fritters, chips (1st frying)	1¼ minutes	325°–340°F 170°C	340°F 170°C
Fish in Batter	1¼ minutes	325°–340°F 170°C	340°F 170°C
Fish in egg and crumbs	1 minute	360°F 185°C	360°F 185°C
Scotch eggs	1 minute	350°F 180°C	350°F 180°C
Reheated foods, potato straws, chips (2nd frying)	40 seconds	380°F 190°C	390°F 195°C

Glossary
Botanical and
Common Names

Alium sativum   Garlic

Alium schoenoprasum   Chives

Anethum graveolens   Dill

Angelica archangelica   Angelica

Anthemis nobilis   Chamomile, Roman

Anthriscus cerefolium   Chervil

Armoracia rusticana   Horseradish

Artemisia dracunculus   Tarragon

Borago officinalis   Borage

Carum carvi   Caraway

Chrysanthemum vulgare   Tansy

Coriandrum sativum   Coriander

Foeniculum vulgare   Fenel

F. v. dulce (syn. *azoricum*)   Florence
Fennel, Finnoccio

Hyssopus officinalis   Hyssop

Laurus nobilis   Bay, sweet

Levisticum officinale   Lovage

Lippia citriodora   Verbena, lemon-
scented

Matricaria chamomilla   Chamomile,
wild

Melissa officinalis   Balm, lemon

Mentha aquatica   Water Mint

M. citrata/Eau de Cologne   Mint

M. piperita   Pepper Mint

M. rotundifolia   Apple Mint

M. r. variegata   Pineapple Mint

M. spicata   Common Mint,
Spearmint

Monarda didyma   Bergamot

Ocimum basilicum   Basil, sweet

Origanum majorana   Marjoram

O. onites   Pot Marjoram

O. vulgare   Oregano

Petroselinum crispum   Parsley

Rosmarinus officinalis   Posemary

Rumex scutatus   Sorrel, French or
Buckler-leaved

Salvia officinalis   Sage

Sanguisorba minor   Salad Burnet

Satureja hortensis   Savory, summer

S. montana   Savory, winter

Tanacetum vulgare   Tansy

Thymus x *citriodora*   Thyme,
lemon-scented

T. vulgaris   Thyme, common

Urtica dioica   Nettle

U. pilulifera   Nettle, Roman

U. urens   Nettle, Anual

Index

127